Modern Kitchen WORKBOOK

A DESIGN GUIDE FOR PLANNING A MODERN KITCHEN

Wanda Jankowski

ROCKPORT PUBLISHERS
GLOUCESTER MASSACHUSETTS

To Todd Davis, friend and hero

First published in the United States of America by
Rockport Publishers, Inc.
33 Commercial Street
Gloucester, Massachusetts 01930-5089
Telephone: (978) 282-9590
Facsimile: (978) 283-2742
www.rockpub.com

ISBN 1-56496-730-1

10 9 8 7 6 5 4 3 2 1

Design: Chen Design Associates, San Francisco

Front Cover: bulthaup, for more information and bulthaup showrooms please call 1-800-808-2923 or visit the website: www.bulthaup.com

Back Cover: Grey Crawford (top and bottom)

Printed in China.

"Island space and safety concerns" on page 20 used with permission of The National Kitchen and Bath Association.

"How long will it last?" on page 26 from "1997 Housing Facts, Figures, and Trends" published by The National Association of Home Builders (NAHB).

"Choosing a vent hood" on page 32 taken in part from "Recommendations for Choosing a Vent Hood" by Blake Woodall, Vent-A-Hood, Richardson, Texas. Used with permission.

"Close-up on concrete" on page 55 courtesy of Cheng Products, makers of Geocrete modular concrete countertops. Used with permission.

"Caring for your stainless steel sink" on page 59 compliments of Elkay, a leading manufacturer of quality stainless steel sinks.

"New trends in color" on page 81 from Color Marketing Group, Alexandria, Virginia. Used with permission.

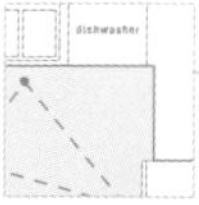

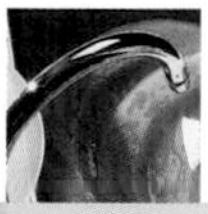

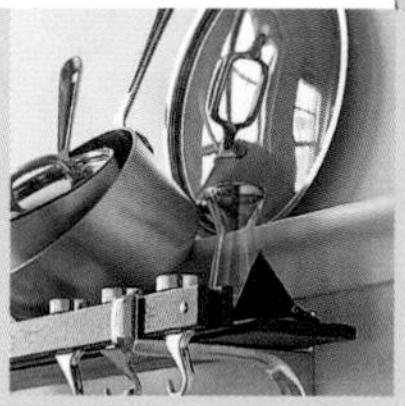

CONTENTS

FOREWORD

by Fu-Tung Cheng, Cheng Design, Berkeley, California

A successful contemporary kitchen...what does it mean? We live in a time of wireless communication, global markets, technical wizardry—times of hyper-change and shifting values. How does this reflect on the way we live in our kitchens? Perhaps if we were to literally mimic the manic pace of contemporary living in our homes we would just end up with smart, slick appliances and take-out food. But just the opposite is true. Sales of nostalgic "country kitchens" have skyrocketed. The broad spectrum of the American public has sought refuge in the past, or at least the Disney-esque portrayal of the past, by embracing the pastiche of moldings and turned wood and patinas that evoke the romance of a simpler time.

Never mind that behind an antiqued, seventeenth-century drawer panel hums a dishwasher, or that concealed within Shaker pine doors are two huge refrigerators. Even the pretense of pre-worn paint finishes on modular cabinets seems to salve these aches for the patina of the past. Given a choice, it seems most Americans prefer to look to the past for their aesthetic nourishment and comfort. What, we may ask, is the reason for this sentiment, what touches them about designs of the past and not those of the present? What is missing in contemporary design?

I think that what may be missing is a consequence of the fast-paced culture that we have embraced. What is missing is what is soulful, simple, and elegant...a quality of craftsmanship, design, and respect for materials that we feel in the work of the past. We associate these qualities with the styles of the past, even though the elegance may not be there. Only the style is there to remind us of the nostalgia, because those cabinets with the filigree and ogees were probably made in a factory along with the modern versions.

A contemporary kitchen is not just a space with the latest, trendy materials. A contemporary kitchen is about revealing the inherent, true qualities of the materials and fixtures through their clean-lined, simple arrangement. Industrial appliances have a specific look and it would be disingenuous to cover them with wood; I wouldn't disguise a modern appliance as a period piece. Allowing materials and objects to be what they are is what makes a kitchen contemporary.

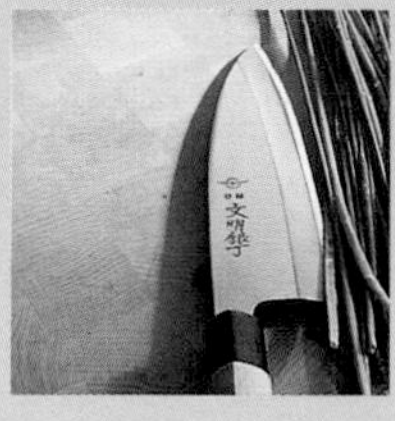

My philosophy is that there is an inherent earthiness to food preparation and there is an almost primitive sense of community in the way people gather around a kitchen table or island as they would a fire or hearth. Modernists or purists may opt for a stainless steel kitchen that looks dramatic, but that kind of space can lack a sense of warmth. I strive to achieve a balance using varied materials that create a sense of warmth and earthiness that evokes an emotional response from my clients.

Finding materials that evoke warmth and a sense of community is only the beginning to creating a well-designed kitchen. Combining the materials so that there is a comfortable flow, a sense of scale and proportion, and a visual balance, influences how you feel in the space.

There are many ways to fashion a comfortable, efficient kitchen at an affordable price. A large part of the expense in remodeling your kitchen is in purchasing new cabinets. Why not install inexpensive cabinets, for example, with touches of custom tile in the backsplash, or splurge on a concrete countertop? Or alternate closed cabinets with less expensive open shelving?

Remember that just because contemporary style is clean lined doesn't mean that careful thought isn't behind its design and construction.

Because I design whole houses as well as kitchens, I see the kitchen from the perspective of how it fits into the entire scheme of the home. Good kitchen design involves taking the broad view of what you want your home to be and carrying that down to the more focused level of your kitchen's function and look.

INTRODUCTION getting to the heart of the kitchen

Redecorating or remodeling your kitchen is a major undertaking, but well worth the effort. It gives you the opportunity to create a whole new look, to make your kitchen tasks easier by building in or improving efficiencies, and to adapt appliances and their placement in the space to meet changes in your lifestyle.

The kitchen is the most used room in your home. It's an important part of daily life for you and your family. It's worth the time and careful planning you'll need to accomplish your renovating goals.

The kitchen has always been thought of as the heart of the home. How many different uses it has is up to you. In addition to being the place to prepare meals, it can be an entertaining area for guests, a socializing center between meals, a place to do homework or pay bills, a recreation area for the gourmet cook, a destination for the family to gather for an evening meal, or a room with a sunlit breakfast nook for enjoying morning coffee.

Many homes used to include both a formal living room and a family room as well as a formal dining room and a full-size kitchen table. Homes built today often feature more open layouts that allow rooms to blend into each other. This casual approach to layout corresponds with the increased comfort and informality homeowners desire in their lifestyles.

Planning your renovation involves thinking past ideas about traditions or trends that may have been the standard years ago when you first bought your home or last remodeled your kitchen. Update your view of what your kitchen should be by considering your answers to questions like these:

- Does your kitchen layout suit how you live now?
- Does your kitchen need to be changed to suit how you want to use the space?
- How many uses do you want your kitchen to serve and what are they?
- What don't you have in your kitchen that you'd like to have?
- What do you have that you'd like to keep?

There's always a budget to be considered, but nobody wants a kitchen that's ho-hum, whatever the financial limitation. So get yourself to prioritize. What are the essentials? What are the details that can wait, that can be forgone, or that can be adopted depending upon the cost?

To create a kitchen that's special for you yet stay within your budget, consider using one or more of these techniques:

- If you like the configuration of your cabinets, how about simply refacing them to update the look?
- Don't be afraid to combine materials. Choose a moderate-priced laminate counter for work areas and splurge on a small marble slab for the island eating bar where guests gather.
- If you can't afford the real thing, seek out moderately priced lookalikes. Stone flooring is great, but

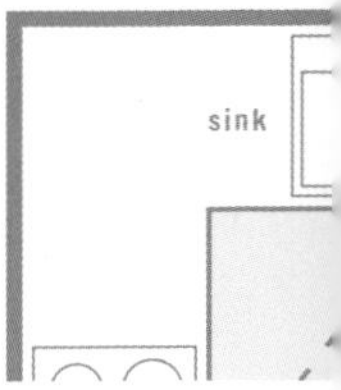

there are resilient flooring alternatives that mimic the look of stone and cost less.

- Use accents to enliven the space. Add a handcrafted set of drawer pulls or a half dozen antique nineteenth-century decorative tiles to accent the backsplash.
- Ask your dealer or retailer for help in using architectural details like moldings and other trims to create a custom look on less expensive stock cabinetry.
- Finishes, glazes, and stain options abound today. Consider selecting a less expensive wood species and spice it up with a special stain or finish.
- You'll need fewer cabinets if you don't waste space within them. Investing in drawer and cabinet organizing systems that truly suit your needs not only helps your kitchen run more efficiently, but can save you money on added storage.

Remember that sometimes an up-front investment in quality products, whether it's appliances or surfacing, can save you money in the long run. Consider the durability, warranties, and service required on items before you purchase.

Redecorating or remodeling your kitchen should be a fun, creative, and satisfying experience. In this book, you'll find fresh ideas on how your kitchen can look and function and new insights on technologies and materials available today. It will help you get up to speed on what is popular and on the market for kitchens today.

Mixing and matching is an accepted way to add interest to your kitchen. Gone are the days when a single style cabinet run is the norm. Don't be afraid to experiment. And be sure to think ahead. Your remodeled kitchen may have to serve you for the next decade. Allow some flexibility in your planning for potential changes in your lifestyle.

This book is organized into sections that will help you explore ideas about kitchens in several ways. The Guidebook section addresses basic planning procedures and ideas, presents a breadth product information that will help you choose materials and appliances you want, and covers what you need to consider in choosing the look and style that is right for you.

The Ideabook section includes ten case studies of modern kitchens created by top designers for a variety of clients across the country, ranging from suburban homeowners to urban apartment dwellers. Here you'll find ideas for creative touches you may want to include in your own home.

The Workbook section allows you to record and organize your thoughts and plans so you are well prepared to begin your redecorating or renovating project.

The kitchen is the heart of the home. Use this book to explore the heart of the kitchen you desire. It can lead to an improved quality of living for you and your family. — Wanda Jankowski

KITCHEN GUIDEBOOK

A GUIDEBOOK OFFERING CLEAR INTERIOR DESIGN ADVICE TO HELP YOU MAKE INFORMED DECISIONS ABOUT REDESIGNING YOUR KITCHEN.

PLANNING A LAYOUT • ISLAND OPTIONS • THE RIGHT EQUIPMENT • CABINETRY • OPTIONS IN COUNTERTOPS • CLEANING UP: SINK AND FAUCET • STORAGE • CHOOSING A KITCHEN FLOOR • TEXTURE, COLOR, AND PATTERN • PAINT: QUICK-CHANGE ARTISTRY • LIGHTING

Creating a great kitchen is a lot like creating a great meal: you must begin with a good recipe, use top-quality ingredients, and execute the plan carefully and skillfully. In this section, you will learn the basics of kitchen design and renovation planning. From deciding on a basic layout to considerations regarding everything from appliances to flooring, we'll walk through the countless decisions you'll need to make.

Consider your specific needs. Is your ideal kitchen one in which the cook is king, or one that invites family and guests to linger throughout the day? Do you cook elaborate meals daily, or is cooking more of a weekend hobby? Will you require a kitchen that serves double duty as a dining room, or that incorporates a home office or meal-planning area with a computer and bookshelves for cookbooks? How many cooks will be using the space? The answers to each of these questions will shape your ideal kitchen design: a single cook might opt for a galley-style kitchen, while a two-cook household is better served by a larger kitchen with multiple workstations. Similarly, a cook who favors Asian-style cooking might dream of extra refrigerator space to stash plenty of fresh produce and a range that incorporates one extra-large burner for a wok, while a serious baker might seek multiple ovens and areas with lowered countertops to facilitate kneading and rolling dough.

Look at the foundations of the room as well, perhaps calling in an engineer to help you assess the degree of renovations required. Is the electrical and plumbing foundation up to code—and up to date? Are there windows, doorways, or load-bearing walls you want to move or remove? Are there hardwood floors that could take on new life with a simple refinishing job? Is there adequate space to incorporate a separate pantry, an additional sink, or a wall oven? Think also about your location. Does your kitchen face a spectacular view that cries out for the addition of a large bay window? Is your home located in a dry, temperate climate, suggesting that an outdoor cooking and dining space might make a sensible addition?

And perhaps most important, consider your budget. Kitchen renovations can be among the most costly projects you can take on, but they also add the most value to your home.

KITCHEN WORK TRIANGLES

Locate the three essential parts to your kitchen design—the refrigerator, sink, and range/cooktop or the work triangle—close together but not crowded, from 5 to 8 feet (1.5 m to 2.4 m) apart. To plan a kitchen for two or more cooks, include an island with an extra sink and cooktop and create multiple work triangles.

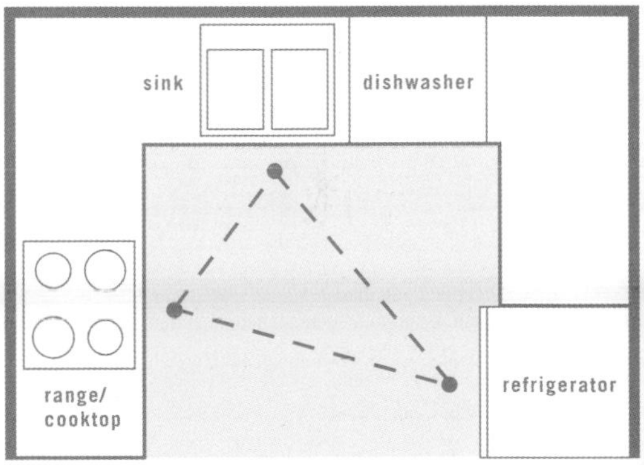

planning a layout

Traditional layouts, such as galley kitchens that have cabinets and appliances running down two sides of a room, U-shaped kitchens, L-shaped kitchens, and larger kitchens that feature an island or a peninsula, are always functional and thus are the ones still in use today. But because modern home plans often feature open layouts that eliminate doorways between rooms, new arrangement styles are necessary. The traditional notion of lining the perimeter of a kitchen with base and wall cabinets might not work in a modern kitchen.

Open plans mean open space and fewer walls. As a result, kitchen designs are heading in entirely new directions.

Layout solutions lie not only with the proper selection and placement of appliances and cabinetry but also with the very foundations of the room. A small kitchen with doorways to the backyard, dining room, and hallway might gain a great deal of space while cutting down on thru traffic by eliminating one of the entrances. A second sink or a mini-refrigerator near the doorway that holds children's beverages can be traffic problem-solvers. Choosing a separate cooktop and wall oven instead of a range allows two cooks to work comfortably together. Open loft-style spaces can house a semicircular kitchen. Multiple islands that incorporate appliances and sinks as well as storage are great for spaces that have lots of full-length windows but limited wall space. And moveable islands that tuck under counters when not in use can provide an extra work counter when needed while keeping a small space clear when not in use.

There should be a comfortable relationship between the kitchen and other daily living areas, such as the family or great room and the dining room. Because most of our waking hours are spent in these areas, it's important that they be designed to easily interact and share activities. Your family should be able to enter and exit the kitchen and adjacent spaces easily—be they empty-handed or laden with dishes, beverages, or platters.

TRAFFIC REPORT

Think about your kitchen as though it were a small city: it includes major destinations within its borders (refrigerator, range, sink), accommodations for thru traffic to other destinations (the back door, the pantry, the basement door), and a population that will benefit from carefully planned routes that minimize traffic jams and collisions. Your kitchen must be designed to accommodate those who are cooking, eating, or just passing through on their way to the backyard, and it must do so functionally and beautifully. That's why it's so important to carefully plan and implement a functional, working layout whenever you tackle a kitchen renovation. No matter how many up-to-date appliances and storage options you have in your kitchen, their usefulness will be stifled if the positioning of those elements interrupts traffic flow and fails to define work areas properly.

Among the most important elements that must be considered when planning a new kitchen or remodeling an existing one is traffic flow within the room—as well as through the room, as kitchens are often a hub between several other rooms or spaces in the home. Key

TYPICAL KITCHEN LAYOUTS

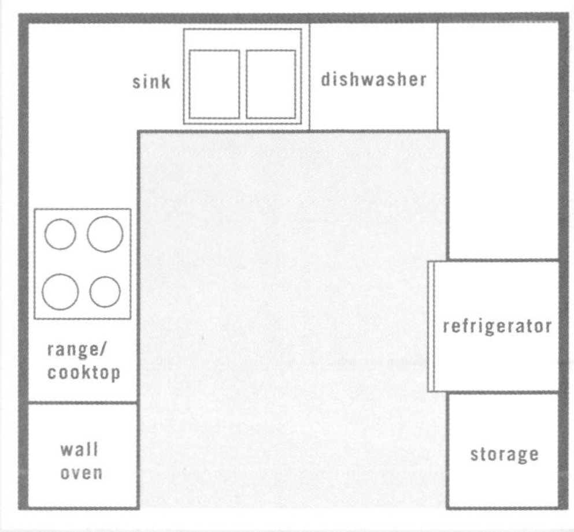

U-Shaped Layout

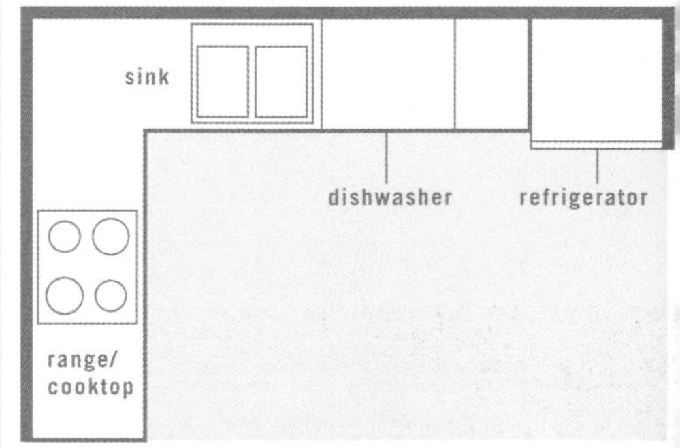

L-Shaped Layout

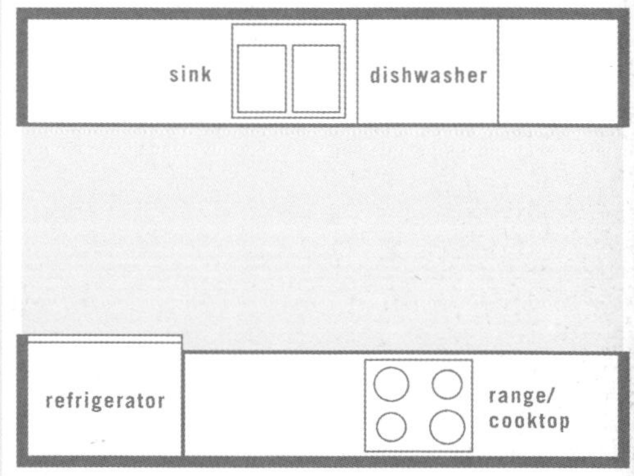

Parallel Layout

A cooktop comes in handy between the dining room and kitchen. Above, cabinets with glass doors attractively display decorative items visible from both rooms.

to planning a successful kitchen layout is to evaluate not only how tasks are performed during meal preparation within the kitchen, but to think about how people pass through and use the kitchen at other times throughout the day. If you are remodeling, ask yourself traffic-related questions like these:

- Is there traffic flowing through the room, as well as in and out of it?
- Are there people jam-ups in a certain area during meal preparation times?
- Is an island in the way of you reaching the refrigerator or sink easily?
- Do you frequently find yourself wasting time and steps walking back and forth from one area to another to get stored items?
- Are often-used items within reach in appropriate storage or do you have to hunt for them?
- Is bringing food to other areas for serving, like the breakfast nook, family room, or dining room, convenient and easy?
- Do you have enough counter space where you need it?
- When the children come in to get a beverage, do they get in the way of others preparing meals?

BLENDING WITH ADJACENT SPACES

Most kitchens today include more than one place to prepare meals, so think about what other spaces you and your family will need in the kitchen, or adjacent areas, that will affect the kitchen's look and layout. A few to ideas to consider are:

- A message desk can be a simple countertop set in the corner with room for a chair to slip beneath it, or it can be more elaborate—with cubbyholes for keys, bills, and letters; a closed wall cabinet to store paper for your telephone/fax machine or writing supplies.
- Your home office may be part of your kitchen or set off into an adjacent area. If space is limited, but privacy is called for when guests are present or a quieter space is needed, consider using a pocket door that slides open and closed to set off the room. Options in cabinetry today allow you to leave computer equipment visible or store it behind closed cabinet doors when not in use.
- If laundry equipment is part of your kitchen area, consider concealing it with cabinetry and adding a small folding/work counter.
- An island can be an attractive way to separate an open kitchen from the family room. The raised family room side can function as a serving surface while concealing the clutter from food preparation. The base of the island facing the family room can house shelves for books or memorabilia.
- The breakfast nook can include a table and chairs, built-in banquette, or simply house an eating bar that is part of a peninsula.

For a more formal division between rooms, consider cabinets with glass door panels so china and glassware can be attractively displayed and accented with light.

- A mudroom can take on a look of its own if it's adjacent to but separate from the kitchen. If you love plants and the space includes a window, install three shelves across it and fill them with potted flowers and herbs.
- A two-sided fireplace can provide a visual division between the kitchen and great room and add a cozy warmth to both spaces.
- The butler's pantry can hold less frequently used serving pieces and pans. It can also be a good place for a dishwasher and second sink.
- Open plan kitchens and high ceilings can mean the noise from appliances is exaggerated. Think about how important noise control is to you. Relocating a humming appliance to an adjacent space, or concealing laundry equipment behind cabinet doors, are solutions.

BEYOND THE TRIANGLE: CREATING EFFICIENT WORK ZONES

Comprised of the refrigerator, range, and sink, the work triangle has always been the very essence of good kitchen design. By conventional rules, the work triangle is the shortest walking distance from the center front of each appliance; the triangle should total 26 feet (8 m) or less, with no single leg of the triangle shorter than 4 feet (1.23 m) nor longer than 9 feet (2.74 m), and the cook should be able to walk in unobstructed lines from cooking appliances to sink to refrigerator with ease.

For generations, this concept has been the core of kitchen design: indeed, arranging key appliances and the sink in this triangle can allow you to save time and energy. But as kitchens have become more modern and multifunctional, the triangle has had to adapt. After all, the kitchen has become more complicated—where does the microwave fit into this equation? Or the dishwasher? Or the garbage and recycling center?

Well, the work triangle hasn't exactly disappeared. It's just been adapted and put to new uses. For example, a large kitchen may contain a separate area for a baking center that includes dry-goods storage, a marble countertop, and a sink.

Open cabinet layouts allow creative integration of all the components of an efficient, modern kitchen.

An island can perk up and add visual interest to a kitchen by establishing a focus in an open space. The added stools create a functional seating area for casual dining.

To plan useful workspaces in your kitchen, examine your current routine and think about what changes you could make to improve it. Think first about the way you cook: How many people cook or use the kitchen at once? Do you need a place to store cookbooks? Would you rather sit than stand while washing or cutting vegetables? Consider also kitchen-centered activities aside from cooking: Does your family enjoy watching television while eating breakfast? Do the kids gravitate to the kitchen counter to do their homework? Is the main telephone/message center located there? The family computer? For example, keeping the computer, phone, and message board within arm's reach of one another creates a simple work triangle; stow cookbooks and recipes boxes above or below the desk for easy browsing and filing of downloaded recipes. An adjacent countertop provides a perfect spot for homework when equipped with comfortable stools, and doubles as a spot where guests can hang out when you entertain. notes

Take note of items and tasks that can be removed from the kitchen. If you have a pantry or mudroom, consider putting your recycling bins in there, along with any small appliances or dishes that you use only occasionally. Perhaps your pet's water dish or litter box can be placed in a nearby hallway to free up floor space. By removing any unnecessary elements from your layout, you not only create additional space but streamline the activity within the room, making your kitchen more functional and easier to use, clean, and maintain.

Because kitchens today are often situated in large and less defined spaces, and because more than one person is often involved in meal preparation, a trend is growing to establish a collection of work zones in the kitchen that form small triangles to create areas where specific tasks can be performed.

Your floor plan will need to address the individual needs of your lifestyle by creating spaces devoted to specific purposes, making accommodations for overlapping functions, and working them into the overall design.

The options for islands are limitless. What kind you choose to include in your kitchen will depend upon the space available, the functions you want it to fulfill, and your budget.

island options

If there's one thing more in demand in the kitchen than floor space, it's counter space. With the popularity of open kitchens, which by nature offer less counter space around the perimeter of a room, kitchen islands are a useful feature for adding counter space and creating functional workspaces within very large rooms.

After all, kitchens have gotten bigger, but cooks haven't—that means that the equipment still needs to be placed within perimeter of the basic work triangle. A well-planned and well-designed island creates additional space for appliances like microwaves and dishwashers and becomes the hub of several overlapping workstations.

TYPES OF ISLANDS

An island can be anything you want it to be, from a simple work counter—a freestanding butcherblock, for instance—to a built-in unit that includes a sink, dishwasher, cooktop, or other appliances. A small, portable island can add functionality where and when you need it. Pull it out when it's time to roll out eight dozen Christmas cookies, and stow it against the wall (or in the hall, or in the pantry) when cookie season is over.

Using a large island to divide a large room into distinct areas has many advantages. An island equipped with dual work centers can allow two cooks to face each other and talk while preparing the meal. A multilevel or multitiered island can conceal the food preparation or cooking elements from the view of guests in an adjacent dining or great room area, while still allowing the chef to be part of the party. Adding a seating area continues on that theme by providing a cozy spot for guests (or children) to chat with the cook without getting in the way. Why not extend counter on both sides to accommodate barstools? That way, the cook can also sit comfortably while stirring the risotto or dicing the carrots.

Consider equipping your built-in island with a contrasting countertop or cabinetry, or opt for a piece of reclaimed furniture—old restaurant kitchen shelving, for instance, or an antique farm table—to create a surprisingly attractive and interesting island that is functional as well. Placement of the island can also affect the look and feel of the room: try placing the island at an angle to the other work areas, which will not only create a natural work triangle but provide visual interest.

Islands don't have to be permanent or complicated—don't overlook the value of including a compact, portable butcherblock table as a workspace in your kitchen.

The clean lines of this stainless steel island incorporated with a state-of-the art cooktop are the focal point of this modern kitchen.

island space and safety concerns

THESE ARE RECOMMENDATIONS FROM THE NATIONAL KITCHEN AND BATH ASSOCIATION CONCERNING HOW ISLANDS SHOULD BE PLANNED:

- Aisles and passageways: In a one-cook kitchen, a work aisle between the island edge and the opposing counter surface should be a minimum of 42 inches (1.06 m). In a two-cook kitchen, a work aisle between the island edge and the opposing counter edge should be 48 inches (1.22 m) to 60 inches (1.5 m). A passageway that's not used as a work aisle, between the edge of the island and a work counter should be a minimum of 36 inches (91.44 cm).
- Island food-preparation center: Continuous countertop for each cook is 36 inches (91.44 cm), minimum. Continuous countertop for two cooks working side by side is 72 inches (1.83 m). The island food-preparation center should be adjacent to either a full-size sink or bar sink.
- Cooktops and ranges: On an open-ended island, include counter space of 9 inches (22.9 cm) on one side; 15 inches (38.1 cm) on the other. If a range or cooktop is angled in an island, maintain the 9 inches (22.9 cm) and 15 inches (38.1 cm) of counter space on each side for safety. The clearance should always be at the same counter height as the cooking appliance.
- Island seating area: Plan a minimum of 24 inches (60.96 cm) wide for each person who will be eating at the counter. A 30-inch (76.2 cm) -high table requires a 19-inch (48.26 cm) -deep knee space clearance. A 36-inch (91.44 cm) -high counter requires a 15-inch (38.1 cm) -deep knee space clearance. A 42-inch (1.06 m) -high bar counter requires a 12-inch (30.48 cm) -deep knee space clearance.

The National Kitchen and Bath Association also maintains guidelines on clearances and measurements needed for other areas in the kitchen.

Islands can draw the eye through the interesting materials, textures, or architectural details incorporated in them. Consider using glass block, tile, or columns to adorn your island.

Islands provide architectural and aesthetic impact. With the wealth of materials and products available today, enabling everyone to enjoy the kitchen does not have to mean compromising on aesthetics.

You can equip your island with appliances or cabinetry to suit your needs. An island can serve as a center for entertaining by including a built-in television, a bar sink, wine cooler, icemaker, and microwave. It might be a new home for a cooktop—you'll feel like you have your own cooking show as you talk to your family or guests through a wall of rising aromatic steam. Or, perhaps you need an island that works primarily as a prep area—you might consider equipping it with a small sink for washing fruit and vegetables, with wire bins below the counter for storing root vegetables like onions, potatoes, and garlic.

If your island houses a cooktop, you'll need to incorporate a range hood and vent system above it to channel heat, steam, and grease out of your kitchen. You might suspend cabinets above the island for storage and to further define the border between the cooking area and the rest of the kitchen. Open shelving above the island can serve the same purposes, while allowing natural light flow through, creating a more open look.

PLANNING AN ISLAND

Whether your kitchen is large or small, the island needs careful planning. Whether you're adding an island to an existing kitchen or incorporating an island into a design for a new one, you must pay close attention to a number of factors before you start.

The size and shape of your island, for example, should be in proportion to the kitchen—an island that is too big or complicated can turn into an obstacle. Think also about the potential for clutter—an island countertop that is extremely deep might wind up being a dead-letter office for unwanted mail, abandoned backpacks, or bowls of overripe fruit.

Placement of the island is also important. Make sure to leave enough room for all the doors and drawers on both the island and the adjacent cabinetry (and appliances) can open completely and with ease. Measure carefully, for example, to make sure that there's room for the silverware drawer to open all the way—and for you to get in front of it to pull the drawers open. Keep in mind also that the island should not intersect the primary work triangle by more than 1 foot (30.48 cm).

HERE ARE SOME PRACTICAL WAYS ISLANDS CAN BE USED TO HELP MAKE YOUR KITCHEN MORE EFFICIENT AND FUNCTIONAL:

- Use a simple island to provide additional counter space.
- In a large kitchen, include a second sink in the island with counter space on one or both sides.
- Stock the island with a range of appliances, such as a dishwasher, range, cooktop, microwave, or ovens in a kitchen where wall space is at a premium.
- Include a raised counter to serve as a snack bar with accompanying seating to be a place where family or guests can socialize.
- Use the island as the anchor for a second work triangle in a large, two-cook kitchen.
- Position and style the island to be a dividing or transitional feature between the kitchen and great room.

You can double the efficiency of a well-planned island in your kitchen by coordinating storage innovations with your current routine and style of living.

special concerns

In addition to cooking and lifestyle, many families have special needs to consider when planning a kitchen renovation. Changing families, concerns about the environment, and particular aesthetic requirements can all play a role in creating a kitchen that works for you.

DESIGNS FOR EVERYONE

The kitchen, just like the rest of your home, should be comfortable and convenient to use for every member of your family—including the very young, the elderly, and the physically challenged. Universal design means design that allows everyone to be accommodated, regardless of their physical characteristics. You may need to consider building in types of universal design features because of the your own family's needs—if your household is a multigenerational family, for example, or if you have a child with special needs. Or you may include the features today because you intend to stay in your home for several years as you face life changes—young children or grandchildren joining your family, or an elderly parent moving in. And even if none of these concerns affects your home now, they do affect many other people's lives, so building or renovating with universal design can add value to your home. Here are some tips on how you can build flexibility into your kitchen:

- Include counters of varied heights or an adjustable counter so a tall parent and a child can work in the kitchen in equal comfort.
- When choosing your light fixtures, consider the age and visual capabilities of the members of your household. Remember that around age forty, the eyes begin to require higher light levels to see what younger eyes can with less light. So consider including dimmers and more than one switchable lighting system in the kitchen to provide more light for those who need it.
- Plan counter space in between the sink, range, and refrigerator. Those with diminished muscle strength may find it easier to slide pans between the sink and range.
- Lever-type faucets or faucets with built-in sensors that activate the water stream automatically are attractive and easily used by everyone, from those with little hands to those feeling the discomfort of arthritis.
- In a two-sink kitchen, consider installing one with clearance beneath it for a wheelchair or so a stool can be positioned nearby to allow a family member to sit while performing tasks.
- Raising appliances up off the floor into customized cabinetry can prevent back strain.
- Using under-counter drawers for pantry items may be more easily reached by some family members than high wall cabinets.
- There are many choices in pullout pantries and storage bins that eliminate the need for separate pantry rooms that may be difficult to access by some.
- Choose easy-to-grasp cabinet hardware or install touch latches.
- More vivid colors can be used to define areas, creating an attractive space for everyone that aids the elderly in guiding their steps.
- Child safety devices are available for keeping base cabinets locked.
- If you have small children at home, consider choosing a cooktop with

Who says islands have to be stationary? This moveable workspace is practical and integrates well with the unique look of this kitchen space. It can be repositioned at a moments notice to accommodate future design decisions.

controls at counter level rather than on the fascia where they can be too easily reached by children.

- Opt for a well-placed wall range rather than a conventional oven for a wheelchair-bound cook.
- Wide, clear aisles should be carefully planned, especially for the wheelchair bound.
- Refrigerated drawers may be an option worth investing in to add to the convenience of some family members.

FENG SHUI

Incorporating the principles of feng shui into your home means creating an atmosphere that nurtures the mind, body, and spirit through elements that establish alignment and harmony. Balance of different elements is key to good feng shui—the term itself literally means wind and water. Achieving the balance that is one of the goals of feng shui depends upon the location of each room within the home and the presence and location of certain elements within each room. But this does not mean poorly sited kitchens are doomed to be forever out of sync with the universe. If objects are not positioned well, their shortcomings can be remedied by using simple tools like color, windows, water, and crystals.

Many feng shui concepts work hand in hand with good kitchen design. For example, floor plans that allow unobstructed movement through the room, provide abundant lighting for performing a variety of tasks and include storage that offers efficient organization make good feng shui sense as well as good design sense. These properties directly affect the positive flow of energy and make the space feel more restful and enjoyable.

Because the kitchen contains both fire and water elements, within the philosophy of feng shui, it can be a tricky place to achieve balance. Here are some quick tips on what to avoid:

- Water puts out fire, so avoid placing the range next to the refrigerator or sink.
- The location of the range or sink should not require the cook to turn his or her back to the entrance of the kitchen. Practical design solutions include mirroring backsplashes or walls. Bells and wind chimes can also alert the cook when a visitor enters or leaves the room.

Here are some easy ways to incorporate positive energy into your kitchen:

- Use natural elements like copper pots.
- Vases filled with flowers or pots of fresh herbs in a window box above the sink invigorate the room.
- Bowls of fresh fruit create a sense of welcome and hospitality.
- Include features that appeal to the sense of smell, such as potpourri or scented water.

THE EARTH-FRIENDLY KITCHEN

The kitchen is one area where green-minded families can put their ideals to work. While recycling, composting, and using earth-friendly cleaning products can make a difference on a day-to-day basis, some of the decisions you make when you design or renovate your kitchen can also make an impact on the environment.

The best way to make certain you are getting environmentally friendly products for your home is to research the manufacturer either through your retailer or design professional. Of course, practicing water and energy conservation goes beyond the products you choose and involves taking personal responsibility for making sure that you and your family use only what you need, and that you keep appliances and faucets in good repair.

Here are a few areas where your choices can make a difference during your kitchen renovation:

- Demolition. What to do with all those old kitchen appliances, that dumpster full of drywall and plaster? Contact your local recycling center for tips on properly disposing of the freon in your old fridge, and look into salvage companies that can cart away your old cabinets for reuse. Make sure that any lead paint or asbestos are disposed of properly.
- Recycling and composting. Be sure that your new kitchen design incorporates an area to sort recycling, and be vigilant about composting. A small, deodorized canister on your countertop can be used to transport kitchen scraps to the backyard heap or bin.
- Energy Star ratings for appliances. The U.S. Environmental Protection Agency (EPA) and the U.S. Department of Energy (DOE) have created the Energy Star label program to promote energy conservation. Many well-known appliance brands have earned the Energy Star designation, which is awarded to models that meet or exceed government efficiency standards for kitchen appliances. Before you purchase, check the appliance's labeling in the retail center or showroom you visit, or contact the manufacturer for information on the energy efficiency of the refrigerator, dishwasher, or clothes washer you have in mind.
- The dishwasher. In terms of water and energy usage, an automatic dishwasher is far more efficient than washing dishes by hand. You can save even more by finding a

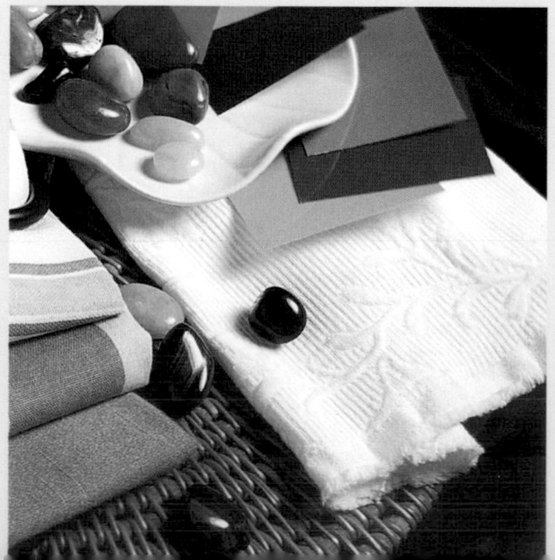

machine that doesn't require pre-rinsing, only running the machine when it's completely full, and only using the cycles that you need (eliminating the heat drying cycle, for example).

- Refrigerators. In addition to purchasing a model with a good energy rating, look for features like mini-doors that allow you to get to items you need most often—milk and soft drinks, for example—without constantly opening the main door and allowing cold air to escape. Or, if space and budget allow, consider installing a refrigerated drawer or mini refrigerator in the kitchen or family room for beverages.
- Waste pipes. Take a look all the water that goes down your kitchen drain, and then consider how much it takes to water your lawn. Wouldn't it be great to get them together? With a bit of planning, you can have the "gray water," that is the runoff from your kitchen sink, dishwasher, and clothes washer—channeled out of the house to be reused to water your lawn and garden. Just be sure to use only earth-friendly soaps and detergents.
- Countertops and flooring. There is an abundance of choices today in countertop and flooring products that are made from natural materials. Be certain that all wood products come from sustainable sources, or look for recycled vintage lumber. Consider also countertops made from recycled materials, like glass tile.
- Cabinetry. Some types of particleboard, which is the base of many cabinets and sometimes used as subflooring, can continually emit formaldehyde gas from the glue that holds the wood together. Several cabinetry firms, feature non-formaldehyde-based cabinetry that incorporates materials held together with nontoxic glue. Advancements in engineering have also led to the introduction of panels and boards made from wheat straw, sugar cane and other agricultural crops. These products are engineered to meet or exceed performance standards of industrial-grade particleboard. You are not likely to notice a visible difference with these crop-based boards, but they are more lightweight than their traditional counterparts and less expensive.

how long will it last?

The type of material and quality of the product can influence how long it lasts in your home. To help you plan ahead, here is a sampling of life expectancies for different products and materials used in the kitchen and bath.

Item	**Life Span (Years)**
Appliances	
Dishwasher	10
Dryer	10
Freezer (compact)	12
Freezer (standard)	16
Microwave oven	11
Range (electric)	17
Range (gas)	19
Range (high oven, gas)	14
Refrigerator (compact)	14
Refrigerator (standard)	17
Washer (automatic and compact)	13
Exhaust fan	20
Cabinetry	15–20
Countertops	
Laminate	10–15
Ceramic tile (high grade)	Lifetime
Wood/butcherblock or granite	20+
Floors	
Oak, pine, or slate flagstone	Lifetime
Vinyl sheet or tile	minimum 20–30
Terrazzo	Lifetime
Carpeting	11
Marble	Lifetime+
Sink	
Enamel steel	5–10
Enamel cast iron (porcelain)	25–30
Plumbing	
Waste pipe (concrete)	50–100
Waste pipe (cast iron)	75–100
Low-quality faucet	13–15
High-quality faucet	15–20

the right equipment: appliances

Choosing the tools with which to equip your new kitchen is one of the most exciting phases of kitchen renovation. From the plumbing to the appliances, every item you choose will affect the look of your kitchen, the cost of your renovation, and finally, the ease and sense of adventure with which you prepare your family's meals.

Stainless steel, black, and white are the most popular looks in appliances; they look thoroughly modern, and their neutral colors will match whatever kitchen makeovers you might undertake down the road.

It's important to determine what your needs are and to make firm decisions about appliances long before you finalize any other kitchen plans. Your choices will affect virtually every aspect of your kitchen-from necessary changes to electrical systems and plumbing to the size and positioning of cabinetry. Be sure to have complete measurements for all your appliances, along with their electrical and plumbing requirements, ready when you're getting down to the nitty-gritty of your kitchen design. If you waited until everything's finished before picking out your refrigerator, for instance, you might wind up having to remove cabinetry to make it fit, or rip out walls to add a water line to the icemaker. Here are some other practical factors to consider before you buy:

- If you share meal preparation with another person, install a separate oven and cooktop, positioning them to avoid traffic jams between cooks.
- If your kitchen is small, opt for a range with cooktop and oven in one.
- Though they look industrial and sleek in stainless steel finishes, professional-style appliances are more expensive and heavier than standard residential ranges. Professional-style appliances in the home also require additional safety features. Most new models incorporate child-resistant controls and extra heat insulation to keep the chassis cooler.
- Take care to vent commercial- or professional-style appliances adequately. Undersized venting for a big gas range, for example, can fill your home with pollutants. On the other hand, an oversized blower may cause backdrafting of a furnace or fireplace unless adequate fresh air is provided.

Some manufacturers offer appliance suites—a grouping of mainstay kitchen appliances designed to visually coordinate so that your kitchen has a unified look. Other manufacturers specialize in types of appliances, focusing on options in refrigeration or cooking or specialty products. If you are an avid cook, consider going with a mix of products from varied manufacturers so you get what each is expert at making.

Though style details can vary—one refrigerator maker may offer a unit with a gently curved front, a range maker may specialize in commercial-style units only—there are basic colors and options in appliance fronts that can help you achieve a coordinated look. Some refrigerators and dishwashers accept insert panels so you can match them to your cabinetry.

With so many options in cooking appliances today, the best way to approach new purchases is to think about how you cook, how many people are involved in meal preparation in your home, and how much you entertain to determine which combination of units is right for you.

Appliance manufacturers are offering more flexibility in cooking combinations than ever. This efficient kitchen layout allows for maximum productivity without sacrificing style.

While they are somewhat smaller than the ovens in most single units, a pair of wall ovens can be stacked to add versatility to a larger kitchen and make it possible, at last, to have the bread baking at the same time the meat is roasting.

turning up the heat: choosing an oven and range

Some chefs will build their entire kitchen around the range of their dreams and spend thousands of dollars on restaurant-quality ranges and separate ovens; others are satisfied with a simple but adaptable mass-market unit.

There are ranges, cooktops, speed-cooking units, warming drawers, wall ovens, microwaves, and even modular units that can be mixed so you can customize your cooking area. Some manufacturers offer cooking appliances only and others offer full lines that run the gamut from cooking units to refrigerators, dishwashers, and other appliances. The full lines offer coordinated looks. By buying from a manufacturer that specializes in a particular appliance, you can tailor your choices more exactly to meet your needs.

The most difficult aspect in planning how to suit your cooking needs will be in deciding how many cooking units to select. Gas or electric, standard, convection, and speed or steam cooking broaden the arena.

The most essential pieces of cooking equipment are the cooktops and range. Cooktops and ranges may use one of a variety of heat sources, including open-air gas, sealed gas, electric coil, ceramic glass with electric elements, and ceramic glass with halogen elements. On the other hand, electric elements can cycle on and off in milliseconds, resulting in more even heating and better cooking performance.

Be sure to note the heating capacity of every unit you consider, and compare it to your cooking needs. A Btu or British thermal unit is a measure of heat that dictates the amount of heat a cooktop delivers. How many Btus you'll need depends on the kinds of foods you like to cook. For simmering and slow melting, you need less than 1,000 Btus. For wok cooking, you'll need about 12,000 Btus, which is the maximum an open-air gas burner can deliver. Most of your cooking needs will fall into the 6,000 to 10,000 Btu range.

In addition to traditional ranges, there are commercial-style ranges, separate cooktops, wall ovens, and vent hoods.

Some cooks consider gas to be the best choice for cooktops because of the preciseness with which the flame can be adjusted. In the end, personal preference and cooking style should dictate your selections.

Cooktop surfaces come in smooth versions made of ceramic or glass that are easy to clean. Many smooth tops include dual-size burners (a smaller burner within a large one) for different sized pans. Some models have completely flat surfaces with built-in electronic controls that can be wiped clean with a damp cloth. There are also glass cooktops that come with sealed gas burners and offer low maintenance. Some cooktop models have built-in retractable downdrafts that descend out of sight when not in use. Powerful cooktops and ranges, however, may require more powerful ventilation hoods to expel cooking heat and fumes.

Years ago, ranges and cooktops included burners only. Today, other options are offered, including burners with varied Btu outputs, griddles and indoor barbecue grills. There are trade-offs to be made if you want an indoor grill option, such as a decreased number of burners. You must also provide sufficient ductwork that provides ventilation to the outside.

You should choose your oven in conjunction with your cooktop, as the two main options are for an all-in-one cooktop and range, or a wall oven/cooktop combination. In terms of savings, the all-in-one cooktop and range can't be beat, costing less than two comparable units and taking up less room than the wall oven/cooktop combo. Wall ovens eliminate bending down to use the oven, but they eat up would-be counter space, an important consideration in a small kitchen. Once you've made your decision on what kind of range/cooktop combo you want, there are a bevy of features to consider:

- Steam cookers keep foods moist while cooked all the way through. Many steam cooking units require a water line, a drain line, and 220 volts of electricity, though there are exceptions.
- A convection oven (actually a conventional gas or electric oven that has a convection option) circulates air through the chamber, providing more even heat than a standard oven and ideal for baked goods and roasted meats. It can also cook at lower temperatures and in less time.
- If you often sauté or deep-fry, sealed gas burners and glass ceramic electric cooktops offer easy clean up, although they are more expensive than open air gas or electric coil cooktops. Sealed gas burners on a porcelain cooktop are generally less expensive than an electric smooth glass-ceramic cooktop. Sealed gas on a glass cooktop, however, generally costs more.
- Beyond the basics are specialty items and customizing features that can make cooking easier and more enjoyable for you. The microwave has been around for many years. Joining it are new "speed cooking" ovens that use a variety of methods to cook foods in one-third to one-half the time of conventional ovens.

Whatever your budget, cooking, or aesthetic requirements, appliance manufacturers are ready with the perfect cooker for you.

While maintaining safety standards, range hoods are available today in virtually every style necessary to complete your modern kitchen design.

- Some high-end appliance manufacturers offer cooking modules and accessories that can be interchanged to suit specific needs, such as griddles, wok units, deep fryers, and grill covers.
- If you entertain often or have a large family, a warming drawer may be a convenient addition. It will keep meats or fish warm while side dishes are still baking.

TAKING THE RESTAURANT HOME

Gourmets and wanna-be chefs alike find the functional design and high power of restaurant-quality appliances both visually and viscerally appealing. However, it is important to consider the differences between true commercial appliances used in restaurants and commercial-style or professional-style models. Commercial appliances are engineered for commercial use only; they are not intended for home use and should not be incorporated into a residential kitchen. A restaurant range has to meet a very different set of standards than ranges for home use. One significant difference has to do with insulation—residential appliances, including those labeled professional-style, are engineered for a zero clearance, so you can put cabinets right next to them. Commercial appliances, on the other hand, don't have insulation in the sidewalls, so they can't be used in a residential setting because the heat around the appliance is great and constant.

Luckily, manufacturers have responded to the trend toward professional appliances with a growing number of restaurant-style ranges. Finished in stainless steel and outfitted with six or more burners of variable size and capacity, they can satisfy the home gourmets desire for a professional-style kitchen in a practical and safe design.

choosing a vent hood

A vent hood is an extremely important purchase, but it is often overlooked and added to the kitchen plan as an afterthought when purchasing a range or cooktop.

A proper ventilation system pulls heat, grease, and smoke out of your kitchen and home and into the air outside (where the smell of your latest meal will tempt jealous neighbors); without one, the grease and smell of a thousand meals will accumulate on your walls, cabinets, and windows, and your kitchen will be hot and steamy whenever you cook. What should you keep in mind to find a good vent hood?

1. Canopy size: Heat and vapors from cooking rise, so an overhead canopy is needed to capture and remove them. Varied style ranges produce different amounts of heat and require different canopy sizes.

2. Blower: It is difficult to know whether the proper amount of CFM (cubic feet per minute) is being reported by the manufacturer. Follow recommendations and ask the salesperson directly to guarantee that the product he or she is selling you not only will work, but is the best product for the price.

3. Installation: Be sure you get a qualified installer. If your range hood is not installed properly with the correct size duct, there is no way it can work properly. If there are any reductions in the duct size anywhere along the line, the hood will not work properly.

4. Noise: Check the noise level of the range hood you are buying in the dealer showroom. Most dealers have live products on display. Turn it on and listen. If there is a rumbling noise or a motor noise, don't buy it. You should only hear the whooshing noise of air movement.

5. Cleaning: Many manufacturers have filters for filtration systems that can be cleaned in the dishwasher. Be sure to check for ease of cleaning.

6. Fire Safe: This feature is not well known but is available with hoods that use a centrifuge as a filtration system. A flame cannot pass a centrifuge. If a gas fire explodes on your range, it cannot get past the blower and into your attic.

An adequate ventilation system is an essential part of kitchen planning. You must make certain that the canopy size is sufficient to accommodate the size range or cooktop you are buying.

SPEED COOKING WITH QUALITY

When it was introduced some twenty-five years ago, the microwave oven seemed like a miracle. And while it was indeed a time-saver, most cooks were disappointed with its inability to deliver the baking, grilling, and browning capabilities of the conventional oven. The microwave has become indispensable, but not so much as a cooker as a reheater, defroster, and popcorn popper.

But the idea of cooking—really cooking—in a fraction of the time didn't die so easily. Several companies recently have introduced speed-cook ovens that can cut meal preparation time by as much as half while still maintaining traditional-oven cooking quality. Speed-cook ovens are offered by several manufacturers and the method of operation differs among them. Some speed-cook ovens operate using lightwaves—high-intensity light from halogen bulbs cooks food in up to half the time needed in a conventional oven. The lightwaves cook the food from the exterior inward, like conventional radiant heat, but penetrate the surface of foods so the inside cooks faster. Some models use infrared rays in addition to lightwaves to brown the outside of foods, while others use small jets of air launched directly into food to cook it. Some models use a microwave boost for certain foods and can also function as a microwave.

No preheating is needed with speed-cook ovens and they can perform a variety of cooking functions, such as baking, grilling, broiling, roasting, and browning. Are speed-cook ovens meant to replace traditional ovens? Most manufacturers, at least at this time, say no. They are intended to complement other ways of cooking and provide you with another option to suit your lifestyle. Many families do not have time to get involved in lengthy meal preparation during the work week. Speed-cook ovens can come in handy in those instances.

Speed ovens cook food faster. This built-in unit uses steam.

New technologies have led to faster cooking appliances, like this steam convection oven.

the functional fridge

The refrigerator may not be as exciting or enticing as the range or oven, but choosing the right one is no less important. After all, this is one of the cornerstones of your work triangle, the appliance you'll be in and out of all day long (and even some nights), whether you cook or not.

A general rule of thumb is to plan on 16 cubic feet (.5 cubic m) of refrigerator space for the first two family members and add another 1.5 cubic feet (.04 cubic m) for each additional member. If you think your family will be growing in the coming years, opt for a larger fridge.

Review your floor plan as well. Conventional refrigerators that are not built-ins can project 5 to 9 inches (12.7 to 22.86 cm) beyond cabinetry fronts. Is there enough aisle space in your kitchen to allow this? Also consider the space needed for door swings: side-by-side models have narrower doors than large top- or bottom-mount units, but they require door clearance in both directions.

If you use lots of frozen foods (or freeze your own foods), the size of the freezer compartment is important. Built-in models and units with the freezer on the bottom generally offer more freezer space than top-mount or conventional side-by-side models. Side-by-side models can also pose problems for cooks who prepare large amounts of food in advance: large casseroles and trays (for lasagne, for example) might not fit onto the narrow shelves of smaller side-by-side models.

Special features abound on modern refrigerators, ranging from simple conveniences like adjustable shelves to more elaborate innovations. Here are a few things to consider:

- Ice and water dispensed through the door—a real convenience, particularly if you live in warmer regions of the country or have small children.
- Some models include water-filtration systems that produce clean, clear water via the through-the-door dispensers.
- High energy efficiency, which can substantially reduce your electric bills.

Carefully consider your needs before choosing a refrigerator. Think first of function: considerations should include the size of your family, how often you shop for groceries, how often you entertain, and whether you own a separate freezer.

- Extra-wide door shelves that accommodate oversized beverage containers.
- Temperature-controlled meat lockers that chill meat without freezing it.
- Well-lit interiors that allow you to easily locate the foods you need.
- Clear bins and crisper drawers that allow you to see what's inside at a glance.
- Adjustable interior compartments or shelving that allow you to customize the compartments to suit your food purchases.
- Shelves that slide in and out easily and quietly.
- Shelves that pull all the way out for easy removal of food items.
- An alarm that indicates when the door is ajar.

Be sure to consider your personal cooking style as well. For example, if you bake a lot of cookies, make sure that your fridge has enough space to stack sheets of chilling, rolled-out dough. Or if you have children, you might opt for a bottom fridge so that they can get to the milk with fewer spills.

For those with the luxury of space, this larger refrigerator and freezer offer a wide array of food and beverage storage options with style.

For large families, a 48-inch (122 cm) -wide side-by-side refrigerator may fit the bill. Models include electronic temperature control, door alarms, and panels that match adjacent cabinetry.

Many freestanding units as well as built-ins can be customized with panels to match or complement your cabinetry and decor.

COOL FRIDGES

Once you've figured out what your refrigeration needs are, you've still got plenty of choices to make. One basic choice you will make will be whether to go for a standard, freestanding unit or to opt for a model that is (or at least appears to be) built-in, flush with surrounding cabinetry. The latter offers a sleeker look but often comes at a higher price. But just because a fridge isn't built-in doesn't mean it won't fit in. Some are available in a variety of attractive finishes to match today's most popular kitchen styles—many refrigerators come with stainless steel fronts, for example, to match the restaurant-style ranges so popular today.

Professional-style refrigerators and freezers are offered by several manufacturers and can be positioned side-by-side for a heavy duty, industrial look. Another option that is becoming more popular is the refrigerated drawer. Currently available from only one manufacturer, Sub-Zero, refrigerated drawers can be installed individually or in pairs below counter level. Easily accessible and less bulky than standard refrigerators, they can be used in place of or in addition to a regular fridge. When used as a supplement to a standard refrigerator, a refrigerated drawer is a great place to keep juices and soft drinks for children or to store large quantities of fruits or vegetables, which require different temperature and humidity levels than most of the items in your fridge.

Under-counter refrigerator models can be easily integrated into kitchen designs, while tall models can be built into cabinetry for a sleek look. For those who entertain often, a separate ice maker may be a key purchase. Slim under-counter models are available that produce ice cubes in varied shapes and sizes.

This built-in refrigerator unit offers a special lighting system that combines lights above and below shelving and casts an even glow over contents. Clear storage drawers make items instantly visible.

other appliance choices

In addition to cooking and cooling appliances, there are a range of units that benefit from new technologies intended to make your life easier.

Modules like this steamer allow you to customize cooking appliances to suit your needs.

To unify the look of your kitchen, many of these appliances come in the same finish options as cooking and cooling appliances, including stainless steel, white, black, and almond. Some built-in models can also accept front panels to match surrounding cabinets for a unified and unobtrusive look. Here is a look at the most popular choices.

DISHWASHERS

Many home plans today blend the kitchen with an adjacent family room or great room in a flowing, open layout. Though this makes for comfortable, casual living, washing dishes after a meal can present unwelcome noise levels as the family relaxes in the family room to watch TV. Dishwasher manufacturers have made great strides in developing "quiet" dishwashers with better insulation that keep noise levels low. Models are also offered with greater interior capacity and more useful configurations in storage bins and racks for plates, cutlery, and dishes.

The most innovative development in dishwashers is the DishDrawer from Fisher & Paykel. Dishes are cleaned in two separate drawers so you can use the amount of space you need and avoid wasting water and energy. Most of the energy in operating a dishwasher is used to heat the water, so the less water you use, the less energy you use.

New dishwasher models offer not only quiet action and abundant storage bins and racks, but also contemporary finishes, such as stainless steel, to coordinate with the latest kitchen designs.

Take advantage of new appliance technologies with a double dish drawer—a dishwasher with two separate drawers. Dish drawers allow you to clean dishes in two separate compartments, saving both space and energy.

DISPOSERS AND COMPACTORS

Disposers mount in sink drains and grind all but the hardest food waste so it can be carried away through the water drain lines. They are generally not recommended for homes with septic systems. Models vary in size, power, and price, with the heavy-duty units capable of handling larger loads and harder food wastes. Another distinction is between continuous-feed disposers that are wired to wall switches, and batch-feed models with drain caps that, when locked into position, turn the machines on.

WASHERS AND DRYERS

Laundry appliances can be installed in a variety of places. Some people may prefer to set an area aside in the basement or in a hallway off near the bedrooms and baths. Some homes include a mud or laundry room near the kitchen but separate from it. Other layouts include an alcove for laundry equipment adjacent to or just off the kitchen.

The big news in today's washers and dryers are the options available through electronic and digital control panels. The number of combinations in cycles and time settings allows you to customize the washing process to the load. There are also variations in methods manufacturers offer to agitate or move the clothing in the drum. The most recent introduction is the Calypso unit from Kenmore that uses a wash-plate and wave-like motion to life and bounce clothes through the soapy water. Many energy-efficient units are also available today, allowing you to save on energy bills and use an environmentally sound product at the same time.

ICE MAKERS

Though many refrigerator models offer ice in built-in, through-the-door dispensers, you can opt to include an ice maker in your kitchen or family room wet bar area if you enjoy entertaining often.

Environmentally friendly and energy-efficient washers and dryers use less water and power and are built to last longer.

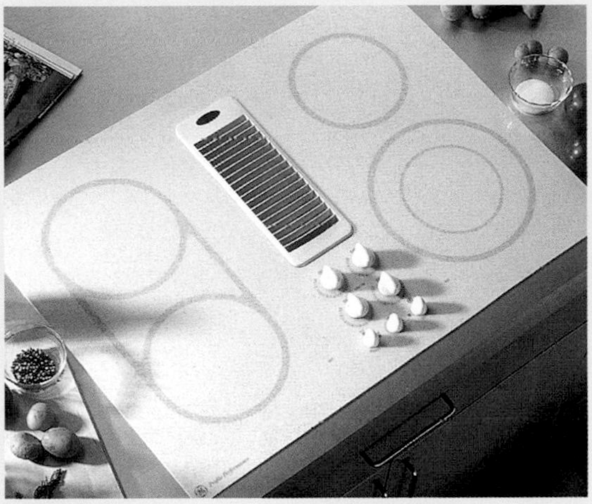

An over-the-range microwave oven with a built-in sensor that automatically calculates and adjusts heat levels and cooking time makes a perfect addition to a busy kitchen.

cabinetry

If the brawn of the kitchen is in its appliances, the brains of the operation—along with the beauty—lay in its cabinetry.

Award-winning layouts, such as this kitchen, are within reach by selecting one or two customized features. Having the island made of stainless steel, rather than matching the cabinets, immediately sets this workspace apart.

Your cabinets provide your kitchen with a huge degree of visual impact; they create storage solutions; and they integrate your appliances with the rest of the room. Cabinetry can eat up half of your kitchen budget, so you want to make an informed decision that you'll be happy with for years to come.

You will use them every day, so selecting durable, attractive cabinetry should be a top priority. You will be considering varied sizes and shapes of cabinets, such as wall cabinets, which are those attached to the upper portion of the wall; base cabinets, which rest on the floor and rise to about waist level; and tall cabinets, which run from the floor up 5 feet (1.52 m) and more.

There are three kinds of cabinetry: custom, stock, and semicustom. The most expensive option, custom cabinetry, is made to fit the specific layout and desired "look" or "style" of a kitchen, with virtually any shape and size units. The options in materials, finishes, interior options, and detailing are unlimited. Custom cabinets can be made by a local cabinet shop, on-site by a builder, or by a large cabinet manufacturer.

Stock cabinets come in standard sizes that increase in 3-inch (7.62 cm) increments, from a 9-inch (22.86 cm) -wide unit designed for trays to a 48-inch (1.22 m) -wide sink or other base cabinet. Stock wall cabinets measure a standard 12 inches (30.48 cm) deep; base cabinets, 24 inches (60.96 cm) deep. Sometimes filler panels must be used to "fill in" space that doesn't fit within the 3-inch (7.62 cm) -increment sizes of stock cabinets. Mass produced stock lines offer fewer material, finish, and interior options than custom units and are usually less expensive than semicustom or custom units.

Semicustom cabinetry offers the benefits of factory-custom units at a moderate price. Manufacturers that offer semicustom cabinetry usually offer choices in finish, material, and ornamentation that give mass-produced components a customized look.

All three types of cabinetry range from solid wood to painted particleboard. Although it's not necessary to pay for an entire cabinet made out of solid oak, cherry, or whatever wood you prefer, all the parts that show—doors, drawer fronts, face frames, and side or end

Modular cabinets with a smooth stainless steel finish enclose appliances to give them a unified look.

Frameless cabinets use concealed hinges and have a clean look. The absence of the frame gives you an unobstructed view of the interior and can make reaching items stored inside easier.

Creative storage options personalize this kitchen for the homeowner. The wide range of materials available for today's planners makes signature design concepts attainable.

panels—should be constructed of the same wood species, ideally with matching grain patterns. Any wood finish—including paints and enamels—should have a consistent look and smooth feel without lumps or roughness from trapped dirt or dust.

Lacquered cabinetry can have a high-gloss finish, is great for creating bold colored and dramatic looks, but is expensive and needs to be treated with care to avoid chipping or denting. If you live with children or just want a durable finish, your best choice may be high-pressure laminate, a thick, durable sheet material that's glued to a particleboard substrate. A less costly option is melamine, a low-pressure laminate that's flowed onto the particleboard and is not as hard as high-pressure laminate. Style-wise, laminates are appropriate for creating a clean, contemporary look.

Another distinction to consider when choosing cabinetry centers on the way the door is attached to the cabinet box. In frameless cabinetry, the doors are hinged directly onto the cabinet box, rather than to a face frame, so doors or drawer fronts almost touch in what's called "full-overlay" style. For a more traditional look, consider framed cabinets, on which the doors are hinged to frames, leaving a gap visible between doors and drawers that reveal parts of the frames.

CHOOSING A WOOD SPECIES

Red and white oak are still two of the most popular woods used in moderate-priced cabinetry. Also in demand but more costly are cherry and maple. Pine, although a softer wood not well suited for extremely heavy-duty use, is great for creating country looks.

Manufacturers today, especially those that offer higher-priced custom cabinetry, are making exotic species, such as wenge and anigre, available. Quartersawn red oak is well suited for creating a grainy, yet simple-lined Arts and Crafts style. Bird's-eye maple is great for contemporary looks that have a touch of Art Deco.

Natural wood finishes let the grain show through; they should be reserved for fine-quality woods.

Choosing your cabinets should be a careful process. The wood you choose can be influenced by what style you want your kitchen to be.

GOOD WOODS

	Wood Type	Characteristics and Relative Expense
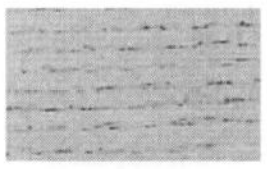	Ash	Similar to white oak with yellow coloration; moderate
	Beech	Reddish brown heartwood with pale white sapwood; expensive
	Birch	White sapwood with reddish brown heartwood and fine grain with curly or wavy pattern; expensive
	Bubinga	African wood with horizontal texture; expensive (limited availability)
	Cherry	Red brown color with satiny finish, quartersawn for unique figures and grains; moderate to expensive
	Chestnut	Due to disease, nearly extinct. All lumber is from dead timber. Market with worm holes, also known as wormy chestnut, rich gray brown; very expensive
	Mahogany	Dark reddish brown, striped in quartersawn sometimes with curl, blister features; moderate to expensive
	Maple	Creamy white to reddish brown with uniform grain. Texture sometimes shows bird's eye, curly quilted, fiddleback, or wavy grains; moderate to expensive
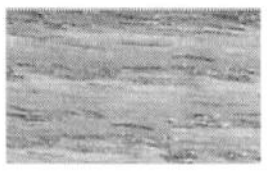	Red Oak	Reddish tone, more porous than white oak. Quartersawn has flake patterning: tiger oak, tiger eyes, or butterflies; moderate to expensive
	White Oak	Light brown occasionally with gray or pink tones, resistant to insects quartersawn for long, light-reflecting patterns; moderate
	Pine	Light yellow/orange to reddish brown or yellowish brown patterns range from clear to knotty; moderate to expensive
	Poplar	Pale brown alternative to pine; moderate
	Walnut	Dark brown to purplish black with straight, burled, or curly grains; moderate to expensive
	Wenge	Almost black with alternate layers of light and dark; expensive

CUSTOMIZING IS IN THE DETAILS

The growing interest by homeowners in personalizing their kitchens has led many cabinetry manufacturers to offer more options in finishes, glazes, wood species, and architectural details and ornaments. The abundance of options is blurring the lines between true custom cabinets and semi stock or stock cabinets that have customized looks. You don't need a large budget to customize your kitchen. You can opt to include a special island, a custom hutch, a one-of-a-kind built-in arch that surrounds the range, or a freestanding custom tower that blends a refrigerator on one side with dishwasher drawers, a countertop, and display shelves on the other. With the range of materials available for kitchens today, even those on a limited budget can selectively include a customized feature or two that sets their kitchen apart. Here are a few ways to vary the look of the cabinetry to create visual interest in your kitchen:

- Add sleek feet in wood or metal in place of the usual toekick.
- Use different wood species to define areas in the room; eg. Have the island made of a different wood from the wall and base cabinets.
- Mix woods within a cabinet to add dimension. Combines a bird's-eye maple door with a cherry trim, for instance.
- Mix textures and finishes throughout the room. Contrast a clean-lined cabinet run with a furniture look built-in hutch done with a distressed or crackled finish.
- Fluted column insets and valances can add a customized look to less expensive stock cabinetry.
- Vary door styles by alternating all wood with glass insert versions.
- Combine elements of a stock cabinet line in a fresh way. Create a special message desk corner by combining stock cabinets of varied heights and widths with a combination of open shelving and square-drawer cubbyholes in a pleasing arrangement above the counter.

Choosing the right finish is as important as selecting the style and type of wood. Even though stained to match, different woods age at varying rates and can create unwanted contrasts over time.

Several European manufacturers offer whole kitchens, sometimes in modular forms, rather than only cabinetry, The combination of curved, red lacquered cabinets with sleek stainless steel countertops and backsplash makes a twenty-first-century statement.

The simple style of these cabinets is complemented by a multicolored tile backsplash and coordinated countertop.

Since cabinets take up more space and can cost more than any other component in your kitchen, the look and positioning of your cabinetry will play an important role in defining your cooking and eating space.

Changing lifestyles have brought an increase in the number of wine coolers now on the market, which can be tastefully integrated into a cabinet layout. Many come with programmable temperature controls that maintain different temperatures for separate compartments.

WHAT HOLDS IT TOGETHER

Functional hardware is the components such as hinges and drawer slides that enable parts of cabinetry to move and/or be held together. Decorative hardware refers to the visible knobs, pulls, and hinges that serve a functional purpose, but are also meant to be visibly attractive additions to the cabinetry.

When you visit a showroom or retail center, don't be embarrassed to open the doors and drawers of the cabinetry displayed to see how well they work. Finding answers to questions such as these will help you focus on quality as well as good looks in the cabinets you purchase:

- Do the doors on the cabinets align properly?
- Do the hinges allow the doors to be opened wide so you can reach items you need easily?
- Do the hinges have a self-closing action?
- Are the drawer slides mounted under the drawers so they are not exposed to dirt and dust, and to provide a wider interior storage space?
- Do the drawers slide out quietly and close with a gentle push?
- Do the drawer slides have a minimum load rating of about 50 pounds?
- Is the functional hardware covered by warranty?
- Are the cabinet shelves adjustable to provide flexibility you may need as your lifestyle and cooking habits change?
- How thick are the shelves? While 1/2-inch (1.27 cm) shelving is adequate to span lengths less than 36 inches (91.44 cm), 11/16-inch-thick shelves are stronger and less likely to bend under a heavy load.
- What kind of interior finish does the cabinet or drawer have? Natural wood veneer is common, but laminate offers protection again abrasion, moisture, and stains.

The functional hardware of a cabinet tells a great deal about the quality of the cabinets. Quality hardware paired with well-crafted cabinetry equals the lifetime of the product.

THE JEWELRY IN THE KITCHEN

Consider all the use the knobs and pulls on your cabinet doors get each day. Just like jewelry, you can opt for down-to-earth moderately priced pieces or go for the intricately made designer versions. Prices for knobs and pulls can range from 80 cents each to $100 or more for a handmade piece in precious metals. Decorative hardware is made of many kinds of material, including:

- metals such as brass, bronze, aluminum, and stainless steel in contemporary brushed or satin finishes or rustic weathered looks.
- resins and solid surfacing that project vivid solids or lookalike granite patterns.
- ceramic units that express whimsical shapes decorated with hand-painted motifs.
- warm wood stained or painted to contrast or complement the cabinet door style.
- glass and crystal in clear or colored designs, which add a rich, smooth touch.

There are many ways to choose decorative hardware. See which one suits your personality best:

- Choose your decorative hardware to reflect your geographic location. For example, if you reside in Texas, try boots, saddles, and cactus. If you live near the beach, fish and shell motifs may be your ideal.
- Select a motif or pattern that is reflected in wallcoverings or kitchen window treatments. Floral and leaf designs can complement a pretty fabric pattern.

Decorative iron hardware is long lasting and attractive. Durability is a must, especially on cabinets and drawers that are used daily.

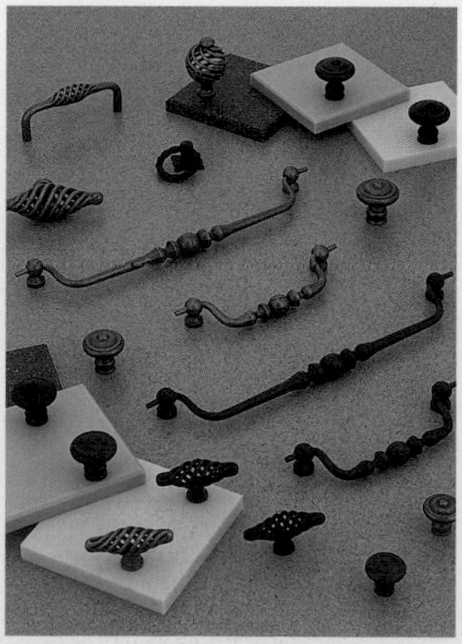

Hardware is available today in a wide range of colors, finishes, and materials. It adds the finishing touch to your kitchen design.

- Do you have a favorite china set? Repeat the dominant color or figural in the knobs and pulls.
- Since the kitchen revolves around food, fruit and vegetable motifs are a popular option.
- Reflect your hobbies or interests in the hardware you select. Dinosaurs, Art Deco geometric shapes, baseball caps—the range of figural representations is virtually unlimited.
- Install decorative hardware that either complements or contrasts with the style of the cabinetry. If your cabinets are smooth, light wood, perhaps a dark metal would stand out as an accent. If your kitchen includes stainless steel appliances, perhaps clean-lined stainless steel handles would work best.

Be sure to ask about hand-painted finishes—do they have protective coatings? How long is the paint likely to last? And when you see hardware in a showroom or retail store, don't be embarrassed to touch and feel it. No matter how delightful the motif or how pretty the finish, if you can't comfortably grab it and use it, it's not for you!

Some frameless cabinetry may allow you to use touch latches that are mounted inside the cabinet door and opened by pressing down on the door from the outside. No decorative hardware is needed if touch latches are used and this minimal look can enhance the contemporary styling of a modern kitchen.

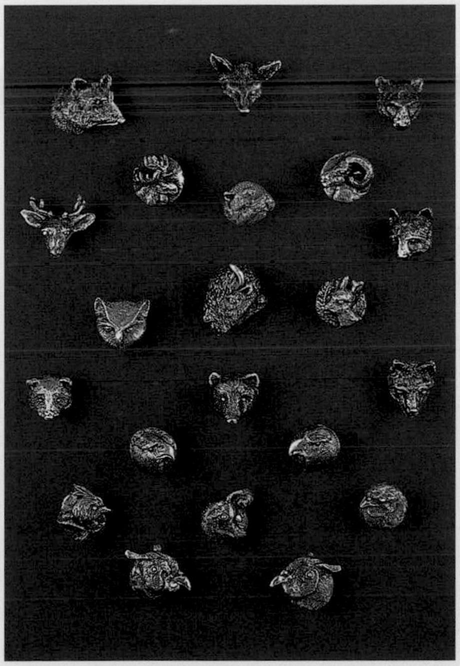

In the past, little thought has been paid to these kitchen workhorses, but decorative hardware can be the defining accent in your kitchen.

options in countertops

Choose countertop materials not only for their looks but in relation to how you use them. And don't be afraid to use more than one type of material throughout your kitchen. Use a durable material to stand up to food preparation and cooking tasks, for example. Then go for one that's big on looks for a less hardworking duty area like a serving or eating bar.

Butcherblock is fine for small areas but is not advised for complete kitchen countertops. Butcherblock takes on a time-worn look with prolonged use.

Professional installation is required for a slab counter. Marble is expensive but worth the investment. You want to be sure it gets installed right.

Countertop tiles continue into the backsplash for a uniform look and clean up easily.

Laminate is one of the most economical options in countertops and is available in a broad range of colors, textures and patterns.

Laminate is made of several layers of resin-impregnated paper fused under pressure and bonded to particleboard or plywood. It can be damaged with hair dyes, drain cleaners, and caustic bathroom cleansers. Laminate comes in a wide range of colors, patterns, and textures and can be used creatively with other materials for a special look. If severely scratched or nicked, it can be hard to repair, but cleaning is easy—simply wipe with a damp cloth and mild cleanser.

A manmade material composed of polyester and/or acrylic resins, solid surfacing is nonporous, so it resists stains. Colors and patterns run all the way through, so nicks and scratches can be buffed out. Burns and breaks can also be repaired. It comes in solid colors, as well as patterns that include granite lookalikes. Colors and patterns can be combined to create custom edge treatments. It can be routed, carved, and sandblasted into varied shapes and sizes. It requires professional installation and is relatively expensive. Daily cleanup involves wiping with a damp cloth and mild cleanser.

Solid surfaces add a dramatic contrast and come in a variety of up-to-date colors that are durable and resistant to stains and moisture.

Granite is a natural stone that comes in slab or tile forms. It is durable enough to last beyond a lifetime, heavy and so strong that it won't be scorched or burned by hot pots set on it. It cleans easily with a damp cloth and mild cleanser. Professional installation is required for a slab counter. It is comparable to solid surfacing in expense.

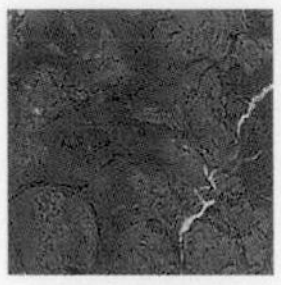

Just like granite, **marble** is available in tile or slab forms. But unlike granite, marble is more porous and will stain when acidic foods or cosmetics are left on it for too long. Some marbles are harder than others, so check with a professional before making your final selection.

Ceramic tile is available in a virtually limitless array of colors and patterns, including hand-painted versions. It is water-resistant and will not be damaged when hot pots are placed on it. Though grout can be susceptible to mildew, the problem of discoloration can be lessened by using a dark color grout that complements the color of the tile. Cleaning is easy with a damp cloth and mild cleanser.

The popularity of **stainless steel** appliances has spurred interest in stainless steel countertops to complement them. Be aware before buying that fingerprints and scratches will be readily visible on a stainless steel countertop. A brushed finished can help mask those markings. Clean with a damp cloth and mild cleanser.

A natural element, **limestone** can be glazed to prevent staining. Over time, limestone can take on a time-worn appearance associated with Old World European looks found in centuries-old homes. It can be wiped clean with a damp cloth and mild cleanser.

Concrete is a new addition to the array of countertop materials. It can be used roughly textured or smoothed and glazed. It also can be colored to suit the décor of your kitchen. Like all other countertops, concrete has its own inherent qualities (see page 55), with its industrial look making it well suited to contemporary style kitchens.

Relatively new to the countertop culture is quartz surfacing. Raw quartz, like the materials found in semiprecious stones used for jewelry, is crushed into small particles and combined with other natural minerals, pigments, and resin solutions to form this non-porous, hard surfacing. Quartz surfacing is very hard and resistant to heat, scratches, and stains. It can be shaped into rounded edges or sandblasted. The colors available are often more vivid and the particles more prone to sparkling than natural stone. Its price is comparable to that of solid surfacing.

close-up on concrete

Concrete is one of the newest materials used for kitchen countertops. Just like any other material, it has its own inherent qualities and characteristics that dictate how you should maintain and care for it.

- Cutting on concrete: Cast concrete is not a substitute for a cutting board and should not be used as a cutting surface.
- Staining: Concrete is about as porous as marble, which means that acids from food products such as red wine, lemon juice, and vinegar, can etch the surface. To minimize staining and etching, clean spills up soon after they happen. But, like aged butcherblock or marble, allowing a patina to develop over time on a cast concrete counter can enhance the look and character of the surface. The choice is yours.
- Chips and cracks: If you strike a corner or edge of a concrete counter with a hard object, the counter can chip (as might any dishes or glasses that bang against it). Hairline cracks can also develop. These are not structural failures, but are part of the qualities of the material. Hairline cracks can be filled easily with an epoxy filler provided in the proper color as needed.
- Hot pots: Concrete is heat resistant, but can be subject to thermal shock if a red hot object is placed directly upon it. Like granite, the exposed area may flake or chip away if too much heat is applied. Use trivets between the concrete and hot pots.
- Gaps between counter and wall: The gaps between the counter and the wall can be filled in by backsplashes. Just as in installing granite, rather than scribing the counter to the wall, the depth of a backsplash can be used to make up for gaps caused by irregularities in the wall.
- Support: Concrete is heavy. Do you need to reinforce the supporting cabinetry below it in order to accommodate the weight of a concrete counter? Generally speaking, no. If the supporting cabinets are single-wall cabinets or made of particleboard, vertical plywood reinforcements may be necessary.

cleaning up: sinks and faucets

The third leg of your work triangle is your sink, and just like every other aspect of kitchen design, careful thought should be put behind your choice.

Think first of function: Is its main purpose for cleaning dishes, preparing food, or both? Will it be the only sink? Will you have a dishwasher as well? Then, consider form—with the wide variety of designs, styles, and finishes available—along with your choice of countless faucets and features—you'll be able to find the perfect sink that fits into your floor plan, your style, and your workload seamlessly.

A SINK FOR EVERY COUNTER

Sinks today are available in a variety of high-quality materials and styles, from sleek stainless steel to porcelain, in a range of shapes and sizes. Determine your needs first: Do you want a double sink? A separate basin for washing produce? A second sink located elsewhere in the kitchen as part of an additional workstation? Then, look for products that are durable and made of high-quality materials. The materials on the market include stainless steel, enameled cast iron, solid surfacing, and composites. Stainless steel (18 gauge or lower) is the top seller, since it matches so well with state-of-the-art stainless steel appliances and also because it is relatively inexpensive. Fireclay is also being used more often, as it is similar in strength to stainless steel, but offers a more dramatic appearance. Sinks made of solid surfacing material come in sink-only versions and in integrated sink plus counter models. Unusual and more expensive materials, such as soapstone, limestone, and soft nickel can be used for sinks as well to project rustic or nostalgic looks.

While self-rimming sinks still dominate in popularity, the addition of under-mounts—rimless sinks installed from underneath the countertop—has provided more design flexibility in terms of shapes available. Though kitchen sinks are being designed with softer lines and rounded edges, rectangular shapes are still the most prevalent. Farmhouse-style sinks with front aprons come in traditional enameled versions and in stainless steel as well for a more industrial look.

Deeper and wider basins have become a desired feature in kitchen sinks to accommodate roasting pans and large pots and platters. There are several styles of double-bowl sinks and even triple-bowl sinks from which to choose. Double-bowl sinks are the most popular, followed by hi-lo sinks, which offer two different sized basins (the smaller of which can include a garbage disposal, so that vegetable peelings can be wiped from the counter directly into the sink). Lastly, offset sinks offer deeper basins that allow pots and pans to be immersed and cleaned more easily.

To date, Kohler is the only manufacturer to offer a multifunctional unit that combines a sink with cooking capability. The Pro CookCenter features a cooking vessel in conjunction with a kitchen sink. This enhanced sink allows you to clean, cut, steam, boil, poach, and braise food. Water is drained from the cooking cylinder with the push of a button. The 8-quart cylindrical, 18-gauge stainless steel cooking vessel resides beneath the counter with its opening flush to counter level. A 240-volt power circuit and a standard base cabinet are the only requirements for installation. The Pro CookCenter comes in 36-inch (91.44 cm) stainless steel and cast iron versions.

As for colors on the market, white and stainless steel are bestsellers, but also in demand are warm tones, such as almond, beige, and blush. These neutral tones blend well with light- and medium-colored wood cabinetry. Black and jewel tones, including cobalt blue, can be striking accents when matched well with surrounding décor.

Rimless sinks provide more flexibility in defining your choice of countertop shape.

A second sink can be a priceless addition to a busy cooking space.

caring for your stainless steel sink

Stainless steel sinks are popular and durable but require maintenance to keep them pristine. Here is a list of dos and don'ts:

- **Do:** Rinse thoroughly after each use by running water for a few minutes and rubbing the cleaned area with a sponge. This is to remove any material that could be corrosive to your sink, including soaps, detergents, bleaches, and cleansers. Most of these cleansing agents contain chlorides, which can aggressively attack stainless steel and cause surface pitting. Rinsing will effectively remove any residue. In addition, foods with heavy salt concentration should not be allowed to dry on the sink surface.
- **Do:** Towel dry after each use to prevent mineral deposits from building up on the surface of the sink.
- **Do:** Scour the sink once a week, being sure to rub in the direction of the satin finish. Scouring across the finish can damage the original finish.
- **Don't:** Scour the sink across the satin finish lines.
- **Don't:** Use a steel wool pad to clean your sink. If a more abrasive product is needed to remove residue, use a Scotch-Brite pad. Steel wool can break apart and particles can become embedded in the sink surface. The steel particles will rust and give the appearance that the sink is rusting.
- **Don't:** Use rubber mats or dishpans in the sink to protect the finish—they may lead to rusting or pitting.
- **Don't:** Leave wet sponges, cloths, or cleaning pads on the sink. They can lead to surface rust.

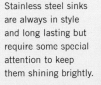

Stainless steel sinks are always in style and long lasting but require some special attention to keep them shining brightly.

faucet-care tips

ACRYLIC AND PLASTIC PARTS

- Foaming bathroom cleaners may cause acrylic handles to crack or craze.
- Anything containing household bleach may attack a faucet's plastic parts. Damage will not be immediately evident.
- Solvent-based stain removers immediately crack acrylic handles.
- Ethyl and methyl alcohol, found in hair spray and aftershave, immediately crack and craze acrylic.

EPOXY-COATED BRASS OR COLOR ORGANIC FINISHES

- Foaming bathroom cleansers may cause delayed softening or crazing of these finishes.
- Cleaners with bleach may corrode polished brass if there are any flaws in the epoxy coat. Damage is not immediate.
- Solvent-based stain removers will directly damage an epoxy finish.
- Abrasive liquid and powder cleansers will scratch the epoxy finish, causing immediate damage.

METALLIC FINISHES

- Grout cleansers, porcelain cleaners, and rust removers that contain acid can damage a metal finish.

FABULOUS FAUCETS

Faucets come in a variety of shapes and sizes offering you not only decorating options but choices in the functions served as well. Here are factors to consider when shopping for faucets and accompanying fittings.

- What kind of handles do you feel most comfortable with? Lever handles are great for those who may have trouble manipulating small knobs left and right. Some faucets come with a single lever that is moved up or down, left or right, to vary the water temperature from hot to cold and to increase or decrease the water stream. Of course, separate hot and cold knobs remain a popular standard.
- Do you want a one-piece faucet or a pullout? For those who enjoy entertaining and need to rinse large pots, a high-arched faucet may be a good choice for allowing large items to be easily rinsed underneath in the sink. Pullout faucets offer great flexibility for cleaning a variety of dishes and pans. Some faucets come with options in spray format and intensity as well.
- Do you have different kinds of sinks in the kitchen that each requires a different faucet? A small island or bar sink requires a different sized and shaped faucet than a double-bowl sink. Arched, gooseneck faucets are popular for use with deep island sinks, while a faucet that swivels from left to right is great for a multibowl sink.

The unique combination of stainless and wood creates a counter space that resembles sculpture.

The style, color, and type of sink unit you choose can complement or match other materials and furnishings in the kitchen or make a statement on its own.

Many kitchen faucets are designed for use with an undercounter filtration system and are available in a variety of styles, finishes, and colors.

- Does the sink accept a deck-mounted or wall-mounted faucet? Some sinks come with rims and predrilled holes suitable for installing a faucet and fittings. Or perhaps your plumbing can accommodate a faucet and fittings mounted on a wall or backsplash for easier clean-up around the sink itself.
- What kinds of special features or accessories do you need? Some faucets come with built-in indicators that allow you to see when water filters need to be changed. Hot and cold water, and lotion dispensers are available that can be positioned next to the main faucet. Pot-filler faucets installed near the range are meant specifically to allow you to fill large pots with water as they sit on the burner. This eliminates the need for you to carry a large, heavy water-filled pot from the sink to the range.
- What type of style and finish do you prefer? A stainless steel faucet goes well with a stainless steel sink. If your sink is white enamel and your cabinet hardware is brushed nickel, you may opt for a brushed nickel finish on the faucets and fittings. Whether you choose white, black, chrome, polished brass, copper, aluminum, or a brushed metal finish, check to see if the manufacturer offers a warranty on the faucets and fitting components, as well as the finish. Read through the manufacturer's literature to learn about special quality and durability features—they can vary from one manufacturer to the next.

Mounting pots makes an artistic statement, as well as provide much-needed storage.

storage

Perhaps the biggest challenge of kitchen design revolves around storage. Finding a place for everything you need in the kitchen grows more difficult as households grow more complex.

Modern conveniences can make our lives easier but they also add to the stuff we have in our kitchens: dishwashers mean more dishes to store; canned goods mean that food is no longer just in the fridge; and wholesale clubs mean that instead of having a box of pasta on hand, we might have a case. Add to the mix the countless small appliances and utensils we have come to depend on—from vegetable peelers to stand-up mixers—as well as the need to separate and recycle our trash, and you've got a modern storage nightmare.

Making kitchens bigger and more efficient, with more room for storage, is one of the key reasons why we renovate kitchens in the first place. After all, your Victorian dream house may have come with a tiny Victorian kitchen—one with barely enough room for a range and refrigerator. But even newer kitchens are often remodeled to make them more useful, especially in terms of storage—houses built as recently as the 1970s, for example, might have been the picture of efficiency at the time, but don't have room for twenty-first-century necessities like a computer workstation or a recycling area.

Storage doesn't have to be merely functional. A basket takes the place of a standard drawer in this space, while open and concealed storage is provided by enclosed shelving above.

Not all stored items need to be concealed. In this cheery kitchen, copper pots are handy and eye-catching and express an individual's style. The backsplash has been utilized to mount shelving for holding condiments for cooking convenience.

Fortunately, kitchen designers and manufacturers are constantly churning out new ideas for kitchen storage. Storage devices, such as sophisticated drawer-divider systems or racks that pull down or out, can help you to prepare food and cook more efficiently by organizing cutlery, utensils, and food products.

European-made imported cabinets are known for their high-quality, detailed storage systems. Storage accessories are often made of steel and may have chrome or powder-coated finishes. Adjustability is a factor to consider in the interior organization system you choose. The Organ Line from Julius Blum, for example, is a cutlery and utensil divider system made of stainless steel trays and dividers that can be configured to fit inside cabinet drawers. Blum also offers varied types of drawer dividers that you can reconfigure to fit any type of utensil or tool you need to store.

A useful trend from Europe is wider base cabinets with more drawers that require drawer slides capable of supporting heavier loads. Instead of stacking plates inside a cabinet, it may be more convenient to put them in a base cabinet drawer. The same goes for often used canned goods and soft drink bottles and cans.

While our grandparents may have gotten by with nothing more than a fridge for perishables and a single cabinet that held all their dishes, glassware, and dry goods, today's homeowners usually need a good deal more storage.

Traditionally, canned goods have found their place in wall cabinets. This slide-out pantry unit, specially designed to support their weight, holds a large volume of canned items, which allows for organization and easy accessibility.

The right interior storage accessories can place your pots and pans within comfortable reach and at an accessible height for your convenience.

HARDWORKING CABINETS

Cabinetry has always been the primary storage element in the kitchen, but modern configurations and accessory ideas allow you to create a more interesting and practical space than was possible in years past with only the standard built-in runs of cabinets.

- If your kitchen includes a large window, consider including a storage bench that will hold linens beneath the seat and cookbooks in shelves on each end.
- Consider building amenities like a pullout cutting board into a tall cabinet.
- In today's larger kitchens, it is important to place storage where it is needed. Think about placing a plate rack or cabinet for everyday dishes near the dishwasher rather than near the range.
- Deep base cabinet drawers and metal organizers are now available that allow you to keep bottles and cans under the counter for easier access.
- Don't settle for stacking food items in empty cabinet boxes. Choose an array of dividers, lazy Susans, and metal baskets to hold food or kitchen accessories.
- Built-in trash and recycling bins keep refuse organized and out of sight.

Other options to consider in interior storage:

- Wicker baskets are a convenient way to hold vegetables or to use in a desk/message center area as a catchall for keys, notepads, and pens.
- Clear acrylic bins installed in your island will keep dry vegetables and pastas handy.
- Lazy Susan turntables for corner cabinets bring what's stored in the back up front with a simple twirl.
- Tall pantry units that install in between cabinets make great use of available wall space.
- Previously unused corners are ideal for including storage units that include varied-sized wire racks to hold a range of items.
- Appliance garages conceal small appliances, keep them dust-free when not in use, and eliminate countertop clutter.
- Islands can hold wicker baskets or acrylic pasta bins that are functional and decorative at the same time.
- Varying the sizes of drawers, from deep base cabinet versions to square cubbyholes, will allow you to store a greater variety of items while adding visually pleasing elements to the space.
- Eurostyle concepts new on the U.S. scene include pantries that use sliding frosted- or ribbed-glass shelves to conceal dishes and foodstuffs. Vertical poles with swiveling metal baskets are ideal for attaching to or positioning near a work island.

Roll-out drawer trays are becoming popular because they allow you easy access to what is at the back of the cabinet. Why not expand beyond the traditional single cutlery drawer to two or three, especially if your family is large.

Above Are you a connoisseur? Including a quality wine cooler may be the kitchen luxury you're looking for.

Right and left Portable open shelving is an option to consider especially in tight spots with limited cabinet space.

If you love the furniture look but want the permanence and ease of built-in units, there are ways to have the best of both worlds. Adding feet or a skirt treatment gives a permanently installed island a more temporary look.

ALTERNATIVES TO CABINETS: KITCHEN FURNITURE

Built-in cabinets fashioned for the kitchen only began to be made in the first half of the past century. But old-styled, "unfitted" kitchens have a certain charm that many designers embrace, using freestanding furnishings like pie safes, cupboards, hutched buffets, and pantries in place of or alongside built-in cabinetry. Using such furnishings in the kitchen provides a bit of originality, versatility, and old-fashioned charm and is a great way to add storage to a kitchen in a rented apartment without investing in permanent cabinetry.

Decades ago, most kitchens were separate rooms, formally closed off by doors from adjacent dining rooms or living rooms. The layouts of today's homes include kitchen areas that are open to and adjoining adjacent areas. If you live in a house built in the past decade, you can probably see into your kitchen from the great room, family room, or dining area. Many homeowners today want the look of fine furniture they've chosen for those adjacent rooms carried into the kitchen as well. Designers and manufacturers have developed ways to create the look of furniture in your kitchen, while incorporating the storage options you need for good organization and efficiency that standard pieces of furniture may not have. Some companies offer freestanding cupboards and hutches that complement their built-in cabinet lines. Or, you might choose to add a flea market find or heirloom hutch or cupboard to your kitchen.

Installing wall-hugging cabinets in different colors, heights, and depths can give a more casual illusion than a row of precisely matched units joined by a single countertop, and crown moldings on wall cabinets add a more finished furniture look.

choosing a kitchen floor

Think of your kitchen floor as yet another work surface that should be chosen with utmost care. Like your countertop, your floor is a hardworking element of your kitchen design: it affects not only the functionality of the kitchen but also the aesthetics. Floors make a huge visual impact, and they also affect the noise and comfort level of the kitchen.

Few floors in your house will have to stand up to the kind of abuse that your kitchen floor is expected to endure—you probably won't have to worry about plumbing leaks in the living room, china shattering in the marble-floored foyer, or tomato stains on the bathroom tile. And don't forget to factor in the level of traffic that goes through your kitchen each day.

From vinyl tile to natural stone, there is a floor for every kitchen and every budget. But before you go shopping, there are a few considerations you'll need to take into account. First among these is budget. How flexible is yours? Will your budget determine the look you want or will the look determine the budget? Be careful when comparing different types of flooring that you calculate total costs correctly for each type, as flooring is sold in varied forms (such as per tile, in square footage). Include installation and labor fees as well for types of flooring that require it, or if you feel you are up to the task, consider installing it yourself (enlist an experienced friend if you've never done it before) and save some money that way. Be certain to check out any warranties: many flooring materials provide satisfaction guarantees. Ask the manufacturer or retailer about the expected life of the product and add that factor into your budgeting.

Whatever floor you choose, talk to the dealer and make sure that it is appropriate for kitchen use. Some materials won't withstand moisture, so any plumbing mishaps could lead to a ruined floor down the line. Others don't stand up to the kind of traffic that kitchens typically see. Still others are simply too hard to keep clean.

Stone flooring comes with borders, corner pieces, and medallions that provide you with the option of mixing and matching to personalize your floor pattern.

FLOORING OPTIONS

Some of the best materials for kitchen floors have been around for centuries. Others are the results of modern manufacturers working to create the next best thing. Each has distinct advantages and disadvantages that should be taken into account before your make a flooring decision.

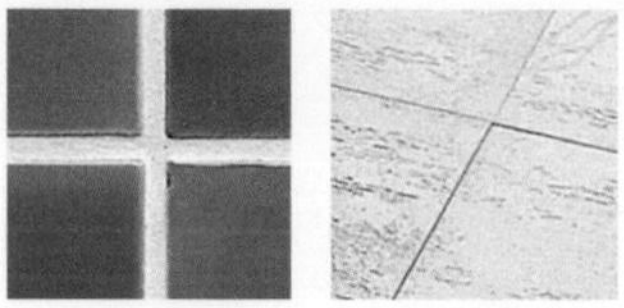

Ceramic tile. Tile floors are relatively easy to keep clean, and while they can be cold underfoot, that problem can be easily remedied by installing a heated subfloor. But tile floors are also very noisy, and any dish or glass that falls on one is a goner.

Stone. Like tile, stone floors are attractive and easy to keep clean—some stone floor enthusiasts say that other than sweeping and an occasional damp mop, they're maintenance free. But like tile, stone floors have no sound-deadening qualities and can be very cold and hard.

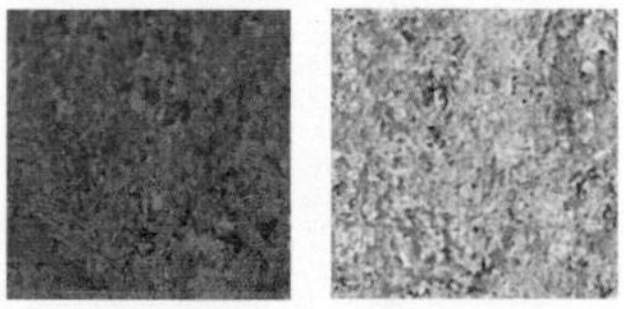

Linoleum. Real linoleum—made primarily from solidified linseed oil—has a distinctive look, feel, and smell that can't be easily replicated, and classic linoleum installations offer homeowners a variety of fantastic looks. Beautiful and decidedly low maintenance, linoleum was all the rage in the United States until it was all but replaced by cheaper vinyl products. You can still get the real thing from Europe—for a hefty price.

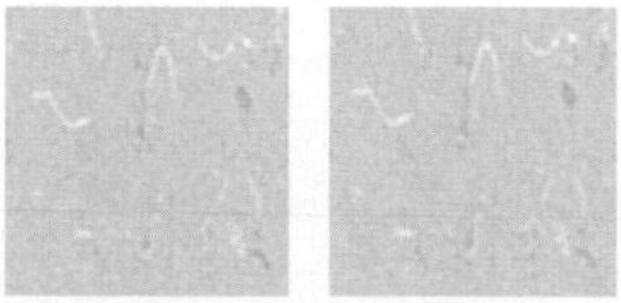

Vinyl. In tiles or sheets, vinyl or resilient flooring is an inexpensive and versatile option for the kitchen. It comes in a variety of styles that can replicate the look of tile, wood, or stone; it's easy to install; and stands up well to wear and tear. Vinyl floors run the gamut from high to low in terms of both quality and price, so be sure to thoroughly investigate manufacturers before making a purchase.

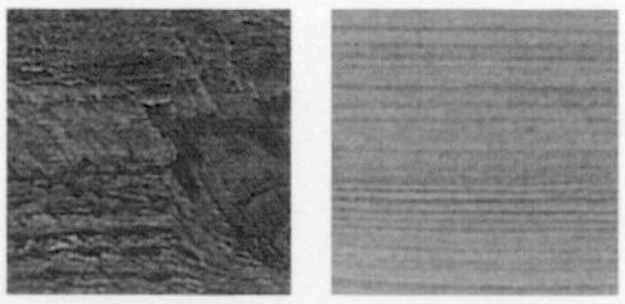

Wood. Real wood floors might seem extravagant for the kitchen, but many homeowners swear by them. Be sure to take care of spills and floods right away or risk a warped floor.

Bamboo. Made from bamboo grass that has been dried and pressed into panels, this new flooring resembles a light hardwood floor on first glance. But a closer inspection reveals a tighter grain, broken by bamboo's distinctive "knuckles." And since bamboo is a grass, the flooring is more resistant to moisture than hardwoods, making it a great choice for a kitchen or bath.

Laminates. Popular in Europe for decades, laminate flooring is just beginning to make its mark in North America. Easy to install, laminates are available in a number of faux finishes ranging from stone to wood. Moisture resistant, they are great for kitchens, but you must be careful: a slow, unnoticed leak from the sink can send water beneath this floating floor, which will slowly rot out your subfloor.

A classic in the kitchen, ceramic tile is available in countless styles, from old-world terra-cotta to ultramodern designs. Adding tiles to the backsplash in this workspace completes this timeless look.

Hardwood floors with matte finishes are attractive, but be prepared to take special care of them.

working with texture, color, and pattern

The clean lines of a modern kitchen are invigorated with the addition of bold combinations in textures and patterns.

Juxtaposing opposites in textures and patterns invites you into the space by appealing not only to your visual sense but to your sense of touch. Here are ideas for kinds of elements to mix and match to enrich the appeal of your modern kitchen:

- Cool elements: Sleek, cool materials project modern, industrial looks. Metal can be used in the range hood, tiles, countertops, and appliances. Glass inserts in cabinet doors can be clear, etched, frosted, ribbed, or otherwise patterned. Glass tiles add a smooth texture to a backsplash.
- Warm elements: Add to the mix materials that elicit a perception of warmth, antiquity, or bonding with nature. Wood cabinets are an obvious counterbalance to metal and glass. Textured stones, such as limestone, add a sense of warmth through their weathered look and rougher feel. Ceramic tiles in solids, patterns, or hand-painted can bring a sense of warmth through the perception of handcraftedness.
- Hard shapes: Islands or peninsulas in straight-lined, angular shapes can add a crisp look to the space. Cabinets with flat, frameless doors and hardware embodying straight lines projects geometric cleanness of line. Flat-fronted stainless steel appliances contribute to the sleekness through hardness of a modern space.
- Soft shapes: To temper the impact of cold materials and hard shapes, add in some soft lines such as bullnosed counter edges, a round table, or a curved cabinet at a corner.

Neutral finishes like white, black, and stainless steel on countertops and appliances will be as fresh in ten years as they are today.

- Patterns: Your contemporary kitchen can gain a sense of unity from repeated motifs, such as square frosted-glass insets in the wall cabinet doors or a descending step pattern in the wall cabinet heights. Decorative patterns can add a touch of warmth with realistic renderings of fruits in tile.
- Textures: To create the most interest, blend opposite textures. Juxtapose the roughness of a concrete counter with a smooth, ribbed-glass pantry door. A copper range hood forms a contrast to a butcherblock counter on a nearby island.

Of course, many natural materials are characterized by interesting textures and patterns. Slate, marble, granite, and limestone are cool to the touch and interesting to look at. But today, manufacturers are expert at producing man-made materials that draw the eye and create the perception of intriguing texture even if they are flat! Laminate flooring and countertop materials and solid surfacing are available in granite and faux stone patterns, for example. Wood grain laminates and resilient flooring are virtually indistinguishable from the real thing, except upon up-close inspection. So don't feel that a limited budget will prevent you from enjoying a rich potpourri of elements in your kitchen. There are myriad choices in every price range.

Keeping an eye on trends is a great way to get a modern, up-to-date look for your kitchen, but it's important to keep in mind that your kitchen is a fairly permanent installation, and unlike shoes or hemlines, you won't be able to change it with every change in the fashion tide. However, today's trends in kitchen design tend to be a bit more time-tested than the avocado green appliances your mother may have opted for when she designed her kitchen in 1972.

From appliances to countertops, metal makes a bold statement in a kitchen. Whether it's a stainless steel countertop, a metal-look laminate, or a decorative metal tile accent tile, the colors of stainless, copper, bronze, and silver are available in an array of patterns to enliven your kitchen. Metals and metal looks are particularly well suited for use in contemporary-styled kitchen where ornamentation is minimal. The shiny, sleek nature of metals enlivens and adds a touch of coolness to the flatter, warmer look of woods.

For a modern kitchen combination, pair stainless steel appliances and countertops with light maple wood cabinets and a butcherblock island that takes its cue from professional kitchen storage.

GOOD COMBINATIONS

The kitchen allows for the most interesting combinations of color and texture in the home. Here, decorative and practical elements intermingle seamlessly, and natural and manmade materials blend beautifully.

- While industrial-style kitchens are all the rage these days—with everything from appliances to countertops available in durable, practical stainless steel—they can seem cold and austere. Try warming up the look with a terra-cotta tile floor, an art-tile backsplash, a butcherblock island, or an indoor herb garden.
- A marble countertop is unbeatable for both durability and aesthetic appeal and nothing is better for rolling out pastry dough. Pair with warm oak cabinetry and hardwood floors for an Old-World country look, or with open cabinetry and beadboard paneling for a retro-modern feel.
- A light oak floor takes on new depth when paired with dark- or color-stained maple cabinets, while whitewashed pine cabinets contrast beautifully with wide-plank pine floors stripped down to their natural, yellow glow. Do you have too many woods competing with each other but you still want to keep that great hardwood floor? Give it a color treatment, liming or pickling it, to break up the look.
- The deep, dark finish of polished granite looks stunning when paired with light, blond wood cabinetry. Be sure to choose clear woods with tight, almost invisible grains; heavy grained woods like oak might compete with the granite for attention, while clear pine or maple will provide a quiet foil for the rich stone.
- Nothing highlights vintage or antique pieces like modern elements. The beautiful scrollwork of an antique baker's rack, for example, really stands out in a modern kitchen filled with sleek, minimal cabinetry.
- A restaurant-style kitchen outfitted with stainless steel cabinets, shelving, countertops, and appliances gets a hint of prewar flash when teamed up with retro-styled linoleum floors and a collection of Depression-era dinnerware.

With polished granite counters, choose cabinets made of wood with tight grains, such as maple or cherry; the light, almost grain-free wood is a quiet foil to the colors of the stone.

To warm up a whitewashed, modern kitchen, lay down a terra-cotta tile floor. The texture and color of the tile resonates with the smooth whiteness of the cabinetry.

paint: quick-change artistry

One of the quickest, most dramatic, and least expensive ways to change how a room looks is with paint. There are two types of paints: water-based latex paints and oil-based paints, known also as solvent-based paints or alkyds. Most paint sold today is latex. Water-based latex paints clean up with soap and water. They are durable and resist cracking, dry in only a few hours, are easy to apply, and pose no potential problems to the environment. Oil-based paints are more difficult to apply and clean up, and take longer to dry.

Varied sheen levels are available as well: gloss paints are the shiniest and easiest to clean, followed by semigloss, satin or low luster; and finally, flat paints, which have a matte finish and are the most difficult to clean. Top-quality paints outperform ordinary grades of paint in many ways, including durability, concealing ability, ease of application, and color uniformity and sheen. That's why it may make sense in the long run for you to invest in a higher grade of paint.

Once you've chosen your materials, from the cabinetry to the floors, it's time to think about color.

Subtle and soothing, sea green cabinetry frames the state-of-the art range. Top-quality painted cabinets are easy to care for and blend well with other design textures.

Adding paint to your kitchen means adding color. Here are tips on how using color in different ways can change the look of your kitchen and adjacent family or great room:

- If you paint the trim and ceiling white, a wide range of colors will look attractive on your walls.
- The intensity and tone of the color can affect how large or small the room is perceived to be. Warm colors on the walls, such as orange and yellow, bright colors, or darker shades cause a room to seem smaller. Cool greens and blues, low-intensity colors, or unbroken areas of pale tints make a room seem more spacious.
- A dark-painted ceiling appears lower than it actually is; a ceiling painted a lighter color than the walls below it seems higher.
- To create the perception that a room is longer, paint one wall a contrasting color. To widen the appearance of a long, narrow room, apply a deep color to the two end walls and a light color to the other walls.

DREAMING IN COLOR

Even if you've chosen neutral tones for your appliances and natural finishes for your cabinetry, counters, and floors, you can invigorate the entire room with splashes of color that speak to your personality and style.

- What kind of finishes, wood species, or surfacing (laminate, lacquer) do you prefer for your cabinets?
- If the kitchen opens out into a great room or family room, do you want to continue the same color direction or choose a complementary scheme?
- Do you want to use complementary and matching colors or do you want bold contrasts?
- Do you need to use colors and patterns as tools to alter the appearance of the room? For example, use light colors to make a small kitchen seem larger or more complex color mixes to make a large kitchen seem more warm and cozy?
- Do you crave a space filled with colors that are in style and reflect today's trends, or do you want a classic scheme that will look fresh several years down the road?

Are there favorite colors or motifs you like that you want included in some of the materials used in your kitchen? Color adds your own personality to your cooking space.

new trends in color

The effects of a global marketplace and a burgeoning economy have trickled their way into the kitchen. Consumer fascination with the colors of the East, coupled with a burgeoning economy and a bit of turn-of-the century nostalgia, have led to a new palette of colors that reflect a new fascination with products that suggest a link with the past and with the global village.

Among the hottest emerging colors are:

- Marrakesh Red: The earthiness of natural dyes used from Morocco to India exudes from this soft red.
- Pink Lady: Soft and sophisticated, yet strong, this true pink will combine with many different tones.
- Sandy Egg-O: This clean and vibrant yellow has lots of personality.
- Amaizing: A touch of red warms this pale, yet vibrant, yellow.
- Copper Blush: Reminiscent of a translucent cameo, this hue is tinted with white and pink.
- Autumn Oak: This orange-based, weathered brown has natural dye characteristics.
- Cocobola: Neither brown nor red, this chameleon color is a deep earth hue.
- Capri Blue: Yellow slightly influences this soothing aquatic blue.
- Silver Strand Blue: A clean, calm, medium gray-blue.
- Blue Too: Blue that is saturated, bright, and fun.
- Black Pansy: A deep, blackened, blue-based purple.
- Lavendare: This pastel purple is pale, yet cross gender.
- Pure Purple: A midrange purple that can be exciting and fun, as well as subdued.
- Glass Block: Inspired by soothing aqua and the lightness of being, this hue is blue-green.
- Smudged Green: Green undertones and a trace of yellow create the base of this warm, dirty neutral.
- Astro Green: Green that is clean, clear, and soothing.
- Storm: Resulting from the merge of mineral blues and greens, this is an industrial and mechanical hue.
- Tuscan Clay: A tinted terra-cotta inspired by the Asian influence.
- Orange Spice: Sophisticated, yet energetic, this orange has been inspired by the Asian influence.

Bold cobalt blue base cabinets create a dramatic look and set off the stainless steel cooktop and oven.

what is eurostyle?

The world is indeed getting smaller, and while that means that we're all suddenly very aware of the huge differences in the way that varied cultures approach decor, it also means that some cross-pollination is occurring, with design styles that have been popular in Europe for years finally crossing the Atlantic.

European kitchens have always been, by necessity, quite different from North American kitchens. The reasons behind this range from the practical—European kitchens are generally smaller than those in North America—to the more esoteric, as stylistic trends native to particular regions make their way into kitchen design.

European countries operate on 220-volt capacity, so homeowners can plug in an appliance wherever they want to use it. Cabinetry is often suspended on walls rather than built onto walls, and storage units and islands are freestanding or on wheels because Europeans take their cabinetry with them if they vacate apartments, unlike Americans. Because Europeans move less often, they are less concerned about resale value than Americans and so are more willing to take risks when it comes to elements like color.

Americans prefer more neutral palettes, while Europeans' color choices are more daring. Americans tend to prefer homogeneous looks and feel comfortable with runs of wall and base cabinets that are all the same and countertops that are made of a single material. Europeans, on the other hand, like to mix things up and are used to living with a variety of materials in the kitchen. They are more inclined to organize the kitchen into work zones or independent components.

A European-style or Euro-look kitchen can be traditional or contemporary. The traditional Old World style that is perceived as European in flavor by Americans is marked by ornate architectural details, such as bun feet, fluted columns, rosettes and moldings, stuccoed range hoods, and stone, woods and finishes that project a worn or antiqued look. The contemporary side of Eurostyle is characterized by clean simple lines with little added-on ornamentation. The visual richness is achieved, instead, through interesting combinations of materials, textures, and shapes. To achieve a contemporary Eurostyle look in your kitchen, incorporate these qualities:

- Rather than striving for equality and balance, create an asymmetrical arrangement that juxtaposes

negative and positive space so that they complement each other. Vary cabinet heights or arrange open and closed storage areas asymmetrically.

- Rely on rich textures for visual interest, rather than ornate, added on ornamentation. Opt for stainless and glass elements in cabinets doors and appliance fronts.
- Mix materials. Use more than one type of countertop material. Include a square of butcherblock for food preparation. Add a run of ceramic tile that can withstand heat from warm pots placed on them near the cooktop.
- Accessorize small drawers with dividers for cutlery and larger storage drawers with metal frameworks that organize jars, bottles, or cans.
- Use a suspension system. Install a horizontal rod on the backsplash to hold kitchen utensils or to support a plate rack above the sink. Add in a vertical pole that extends to the ceiling and supports baskets for fruits and dry vegetables near a small sink and work counter.
- Create specific work zones rather than designing the whole kitchen around a single work triangle. Place a chopping block near a cooktop. Create a baking center with cabinets for storing flour, sugar, and small appliances and a marble countertop for rolling and kneading dough.

The lighting fixtures and systems you choose and how they are placed are affected by factors such as ceiling height, the amount of daylight available in the room, and the location of work surfaces. Consider the reflective value of the stainless steel interior of this modern workspace, actually located in a cooking school.

lighting

You may have the perfect layout, beautiful cabinets, a stunning floor, and top-notch appliances, all put together and decorated with style and care. But without proper lighting, your kitchen might be impractical and unattractive. So it's important to put together a lighting scheme that functions beautifully.

Lighting fixture types each serve a different purpose, so don't go by looks alone. Track lights, for example, usually cast defined beams of light. They are great for accenting the center of an island or highlighting collectibles on a display shelf. Track lighting is a good solution when there is not enough space behind the ceiling to install ceiling-recessed downlights. Track lights, however, usually do not provide adequate general lighting. Recessed fixtures are commonplace in many kitchens, but there are drawbacks to using only this type. Since they project light downward, the ceiling and upper portion of the kitchen can look dark and will make the room seem smaller than it really is.

Hopefully, you have refreshing daylight streaming into your kitchen during the day. At night, however, the windows will become like black holes if you do not plan any exterior lighting that illuminates the landscape beyond.

Decorative task lighting is a great way to provide light over an island. Lighting controls can be installed to change light levels to suit the tasks at hand.

Lighting affects not only your ability to perform tasks but your mood and the way the objects and materials in the kitchen are perceived.

How bright or dark a room appears is affected by its color schemes: light colors reflect more light than dark colors, which absorb it, so a kitchen that is primarily white will require less light than a dark one.

CREATING LAYERS OF LIGHT

Lighting serves several purposes in the kitchen: it allows you to see well in order to perform a variety of tasks, it influences your mood and how you feel in a space, and the fixtures themselves can add an attractive decorative element to a room. With all those roles to play, it is easy to understand why using the "layers of light" approach in your kitchen is the best way to insure you'll have visual comfort, no matter what tasks or situations are taking place there.

Planning for layers of light rather than only one type of lighting system gives you flexibility. The layers can address these basic types of lighting: ambient or general lighting, which provides a soft wash that illuminates a large space; task lighting, which provides illumination to accomplish specific tasks (lighting that shines directly on countertops, for example, or on the range), and accent lighting, which focuses light on a specific object or area for aesthetic rather than task-oriented purposes. Planning a combination of these types of lightings is key to kitchen design. By adding dimmer switches, you can increase the flexibility of your lighting plan and allow single fixtures to fulfill multiple functions (countertop task lighting, for example, can provide gentle illumination when the kitchen is closed for the night). Lighting controls also help you to conserve energy—to only use the amount of light you really need where you need it for a particular task. Finally, don't overlook the power of daylight! Consider the amount of available light when you create your lighting plan. Adding a window or skylight can allow a refreshing amount of light in from outside during the day and save energy too.

To brighten the ceiling area, add above-cabinet lighting that projects light upward. To illuminate countertops, use under-cabinet fixtures. Both types of fixtures can be concealed behind moldings or trim. A creative lighting solution over an island will optimize working conditions and add a signature style.

ILLUMINATING POSSIBILITIES

Each light fixture, of course, needs a light source—a bulb or tube. There are many types of light sources available today. The light source you use depends on the fixture, on what quality of color rendering you want, and on your requirements for energy efficiency (some states have strict energy codes regarding what light sources are used in the home). These are the most commonly used:

- Incandescent. The golden white light from an incandescent bulb renders all color well. These bulbs can be dimmed easily but are the least energy efficient light source with the shortest life span.
- Halogen. Halogen lamps produce a bright, white light that enhances skin tone because it renders a wide spectrum of colors well. Halogens are more efficient, have a longer life than incandescent bulbs and are easily dimmable. However, they are more expensive and generate a significant amount of heat, requiring proper ventilation. Halogen lamps also require a transformer to operate.
- Fluorescent light sources come in tubes and in bulblike versions known as compact fluorescents. Some compact fluorescents are made to fit into incandescent bulb sockets. All fluorescents need a ballast to operate. With fluorescent tubes, the ballast is separate; many versions of compact fluorescents have the ballasts built into the bulblike package.
- Warm white, deluxe, and triphosphor fluorescent tubes render a range of colors well. But avoid using cool white fluorescent, which emphasizes blues and greens in the color spectrum, is weak on rendering reds and oranges, and so gives the average complexion a washed-out look. Fluorescent lamps, both the tubes and the compact fluorescent lights that are designed to fit into incandescent bulb sockets, are energy efficient and have a long life. But it should be noted that fluorescents can take up to several minutes to reach their full light level and that some fluorescents cannot be dimmed.

Part of what makes a good light fixture is the diffuser, shade, or lens that controls and shapes the light beams that emanate from the bulb or tube. Look at the fixture illuminated in the showroom before you buy and make sure there is little or no glare. Glare from inadequately shielded light sources can cause discomfort. Whether or not you experience glare from your lighting system also depends on how the fixtures are placed in the space.

choosing the right light fixture

When shopping for light fixtures, consider these factors:

- The aesthetic appearance of the fixture.
- How its light source renders color.
- Whether two or more light sources from varied fixtures will be compatible from a color rendering point of view in the same room.
- The quantity of light needed.
- The budget available for purchasing equipment.
- The energy requirements set by the state or federal government.

Fixture types that are commonly used in the kitchen include:

- Downlights, which are also known as "cans," these are circular, ceiling-recessed cylinders with reflector systems that are equipped with incandescent PAR lamps, halogen MR-16s, or compact fluorescents.
- Ceiling-mounted fixtures are mounted onto the ceiling and usually have an acrylic or glass diffuser that controls the light from the fluorescent tubes or incandescent bulbs behind it.
- Ceiling-recessed fixtures are mounted flush with the ceiling and can have a lens or diffuser that controls the light from the fluorescent tubes or incandescent bulbs behind it.
- Track lighting consists of trackheads that include the light source mounted onto wire or metal tracks. The great advantage of a track system is that the trackheads are adjustable and can be focused to cast light directly toward objects to be highlighted or on specific task areas.
- Pendant fixtures or chandeliers are suspended on wires down from the ceiling. These are usually used over islands and eating areas and provide a decorative touch.
- Sconces are wall-mounted fixtures that can be equipped with a variety of sources. They provide ambient or general illumination.
- Under-cabinet fixtures come in many forms, but whether they are linear fixtures that include fluorescent tubes or circular units that include low-voltage halogen bulbs, the phrase refers to any fixture mounted to the underside of a wall cabinet to provide light over the countertop or work surface below.
- Over-cabinet fixtures are fixtures that are mounted on top of wall cabinets to uplight the room; that is, to cast light upwards, particularly in high-ceilinged kitchens.

If you have cabinets with glass-inset doors, installing lighting inside the cabinets—particularly if they have glass shelves—allows you to showcase china or other decorative objects.

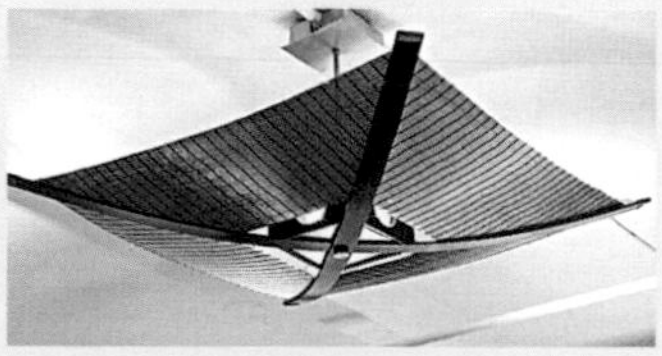

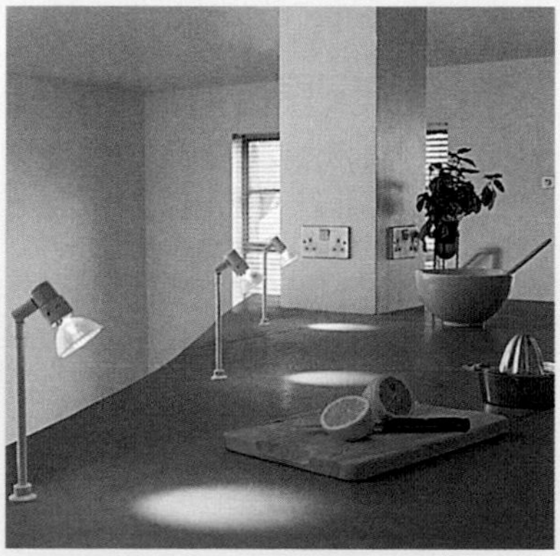

options for personalizing

Many homeowners are changing their attitudes about resale value. Years ago, you might have been afraid to go too wild in decorating your home because if you moved, it might make it more difficult to find a buyer who shared your tastes or lifestyle.

Today, however, the home is a necessary haven that protects and comforts you and your family from the stress of a world that is changing more quickly each day. You deserve to have the kitchen you want, and not just the kitchen you think the next buyer will want! Chances are, what you like will peak someone else's interest anyway.

So think about the time and energy you spend at home. Don't you want some part of your personality and interests to be reflected in it? Here are a few tips on how you can put more fun and more of you and your family into your kitchen:

- Do you have a favorite color? If you want to keep the large components neutral, consider using splashes of your favorite color as an accent in hardware, backsplash tiles, and a couple of inset-cabinet panels.
- Are you a horse, dog, or cat lover? Splurge on a hand-painted backsplash behind the range that depicts those charming creatures with style.

Consider changes from the usual to add comfort and convenience.

- Are you very tall or very petite? Don't be shy about varying standard counter and wall cabinet heights to make your time in the kitchen easier.
- Do you like to read in the kitchen? Add a cozy built-in bench beneath a window with a bookcase at its side in the kitchen.

Plan purchases and make space for kitchen-related interests.

- Do you love to make pancakes in the morning? Choose a range with changeable accessories that include a griddle module.
- The island is a great place to incorporate personal preferences because it can serve as a showcase and conversation piece for visiting guests. Imbed fossils or semiprecious stones in a concrete countertop. Or include a built-in television near the eating bar.
- Are you a collector? Glass-door cabinetry or open shelves can showcase your heart's desire, from vintage china to retro toy cars.

Key in planning your new kitchen is to reach beyond the details of what you had in your previous space. Imagine what you want your kitchen to be. Imagine a space you'll be drawn to.

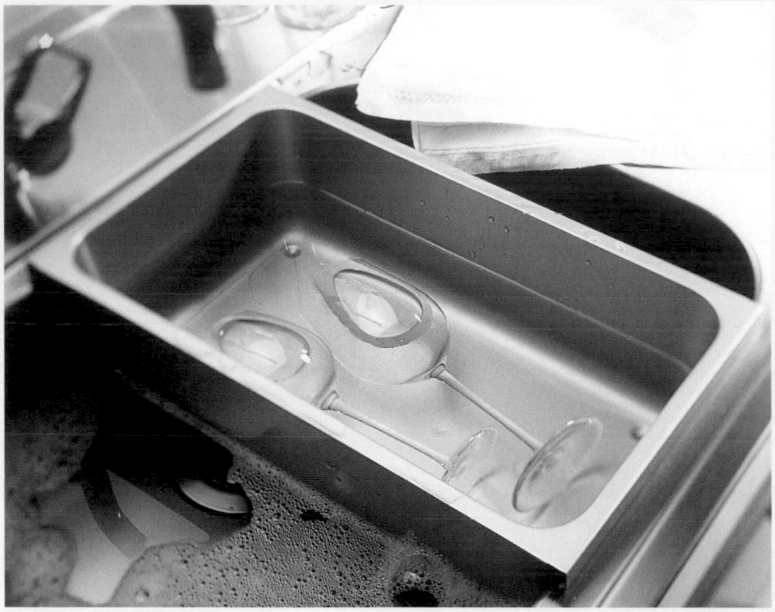

KITCHEN IDEABOOK

THE IDEABOOK IS JUST THAT—A COLLECTION OF GREAT INSPIRATIONS FOR YOUR KITCHEN.

BROWNSTONE BEAUTY REBORN • LOFTY AMBITIONS • BEHIND CLOSED DOORS • WHIMSY IN THE KITCHEN • MIXING WOODS AND METAL • REPEATING COLOR AND PATTERN • BUNGALOW BEAUTY • GOING RETRO • THE FIRE IN METAL • PENTHOUSE PHENOMENON

Every kitchen has a story. Whether it is a new construction, a minor renovation, or a major overhaul, each and every new kitchen has a tale to tell, and in the telling, can provide boundless inspiration for kitchens-to-be.

A kitchen renovation may have been born from a desire for more space for a growing family, or to add a bit of living space to a kitchen that was once for cooks only. Or perhaps the renovation was undertaken to update a prewar kitchen to reflect the realities of the twenty-first century, with modern appliances, conveniences, and necessities that simply didn't exist when the kitchen was originally constructed. And of course, some kitchens are practically conjured from thin air, plopped into spaces that were never really intended for living—like a converted loft.

But even those kitchens that seem to have appeared magically from nowhere have their roots: they come from the imagination and creativity of homeowners, designers, and architects who are able to look at a space and tap into its history, as well as its potential. The best new kitchens offer a taste of their owner's personality, reflect their cooking style, and complement the style, history, and décor of the homes they occupy. Hardworking rooms that make working hard a pleasure, these kitchens invariably become the very heart of the home.

This section profiles ten kitchen designs, detailing the unique ideas, challenges, and solutions that make each one a success. Take a good look at the kitchens shown here—as well as in catalogs, magazines, and even in the homes of your friends—and compare them with your own vision. Use this section to help you come up with details, ideas, solutions, and features you might be able to borrow or adapt for your own unique situation.

a brownstone beauty reborn

By enlarging your kitchen space, you can make room for kitchen amenities that an older kitchen lacks. A large butcherblock island accommodates necessary cabinetry along with ingenious storage bins for bulk food.

When the new owners of a turn-of-the-century Victorian brownstone began their renovation, they decided the most important room to tackle was the kitchen. With its worn-out linoleum, painted steel cabinetry, and outdated appliances, the old kitchen was indeed in need of an update. And, with two chefs in the house and children on the way, the couple determined that they needed more space and versatility than the present floor plan allowed.

They decided first to enlarge the space by adding the room that was originally the dining room into the kitchen space. This gave the kitchen a more open feel and made room for amenities that were essentially unheard of when the kitchen was originally designed: a six-burner, commercial-style range, an oversized side-by-side refrigerator and a separate wine refrigerator; and a huge butcherblock island that housed a dishwasher and microwave oven. The couple liked the vintage kitchen sink, a classic cast iron dual-basin unit with a deep apron, and decided to have it reglazed and fitted with a new faucet system as well as having the metal cabinet below it replaced. They also decided to replace one of the existing windows with a French door that opened out onto a back deck where they hoped to cook and entertain during warm weather.

Take advantage of the latest cabinet designs to create smart storage.

Install deep sliding shelves to make items stored in the back as accessible as those stored right on the countertop.

Reclaim older fixtures to add vintage character to your new kitchen. Instead of replacing an old deep-apron cast iron sink, consider reglazing it and pairing with new faucet system.

The contractor zeroed in on the foundation of the building and the room. A look at the electrical infrastructure revealed a system that was as outdated and efficient as the 1948 Frigidaire that came with the place. The plumbing was in better shape, though some modernization was required. Beneath the kitchen linoleum was a wide-plank hardwood subfloor that to all parties throughout was too beautiful to cover up, although it required refinishing. Underneath the drywall, they discovered exquisite brick walls that were left exposed to stunning effect.

While the contractor went about the necessary upgrades and retooling, the couple began shopping. To replace the old metal cabinets, custom cherry cabinets with glass-fronted doors for the wall cabinets and closed, slatted doors for the base were ordered. But deciding on a countertop was not quite so easy. He wanted natural slate, which he felt would complement the cherry cabinets and make a nice transition to the stainless steel modernity of the new appliances, while she—an avid baker—wanted a portion of the countertop to be made of marble. But one thing they could agree on was that there was nothing more practical and beautiful than a thick butcher-block slab to top the island. A compromise was reached in which all three requests were satisfied.

The baking area, installed in front of the remaining window, actually solved a problem. The existing window was too close to the floor to accommodate a standard-height countertop in front of it, but the owners did not want to change the shape of the window, which they felt fit in with the architectural integrity of the home (indeed, every window in the brownstone's three stories was a standard 30 by 60 inches/76 cm by 152 cm). So, the section of countertop in front of the window was lowered slightly to accommodate the window and to make kneading bread and rolling out cookies a bit easier for the 5-foot-3-inch-tall baker.

A bevy of exciting and practical options were installed inside the cabinets. Beneath the island, doors open to reveal deep sliding shelves that make items stored in the back as accessible as those stored right on the countertop. A trash compactor was installed beside the sink, camouflaged to match the slatted doors of the base cabinets. Below the sink, the doors open to reveal separate and easy-to-remove bins for trash and two types of recyclables. Above the sink, walls were covered in Mexican tiles in muted shades; the pattern would be repeated on the wall behind the cooktop.

lofty ambitions

The couple wanted a kitchen that is fun and functional while maintaining the open, airy feeling of the loft that initially attracted them to it.

The couple who owns this 2,300-square-foot loft in Manhattan's trendy Soho neighborhood wanted a truly functional kitchen. Though the loft, originally the site of a factory, had previously served as an artist's residence, the space has been completely gutted, except for a portion of a small bath.

They hired a kitchen designer who came up with a kitchen that is at once efficient and inviting. The 500-square-foot kitchen is centrally located in the window-filled loft. The kitchen area is defined by a long peninsula of base cabinets topped with counters that wrap around appliances and workspace that runs against the wall. Around the corner of the wall at one end of the peninsula is a sizeable walk-in pantry, which has a doorless entry. The pantry doubles as wine storage and has a special outlet in it for an air conditioner to keep the wine cool.

Tall Douglas fir ceiling crossbeams were also preexisting in the dining area. The designer has enriched that space by adding smaller Douglas fir beams perpendicular to the large beams.

The designer incorporated preexisting Douglas fir columns that are necessary structural elements into his design, using them to further define the kitchen area while adding warmth and a sense of the building's history. The 10-inch (25.4 cm)-diameter columns, stripped to reveal their natural rich grain, are complemented by the bands of copper wrapped around the bases. This matches the copper that clads the eating bar and the copper barstools.

Within the kitchen, varied materials and textures are combined to create visual interest. Counters of durable Blue Pearl granite are paired with a sink and surround of stainless steel. The Jerusalem stone that covers the kitchen wall is a type of limestone mined in Israel. Used in many of the historic buildings in Soho, the designer chose to incorporate it here for its color, density, and texture. The backsplash is formed with decorative antique terra-cotta Provençale tile. The cold metallic and stone elements are balanced by the addition of cabinetry and an eating bar counter made of rich cherry.

The lighting in the kitchen has also received special attention. Sconces mounted on the columns are also made with custom mouth-blown glass shades and are fitted with incandescent bulbs. The pendants suspended over the granite counter also contain incandescent bulbs.

Opposite page: The couple wanted to grill near their dining table and so a wood-burning grill, which includes a rotisserie, graces the area.

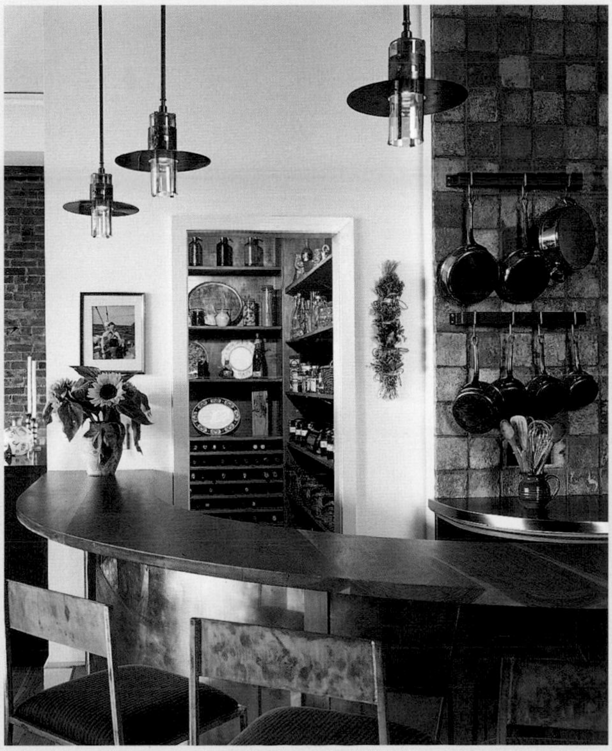

Suspended over the eating bar are mouth-blown amber Mexican glass and copper fixtures fitted with Edison bulbs that reveal glowing filaments.

behind closed doors

When meals are served in the adjacent dining area, the host can close the cabinets to hide food-preparation clutter.

The cabinets are extra deep, measuring in at 3 feet, to increase storage capacity and to house the organized system of pullout drawers that hold everything from pots and pans to dishes, cups, and glasses.

When meals are being prepared, everything the cook needs is close at hand in this compact space. This concealed kitchen is a blessing for small apartments where space is limited, as well as for larger homes in which the kitchen area is open to the great room.

This owner of this 120-square-foot New York apartment kitchen was conceived by its interior-designer owner who wanted a space that was functional, but in which none of the workaday clutter of kitchen life would be visible to guests.

What guests do see is a functional island, made with a black granite countertop and circular, satin-finish stainless steel support columns. The island includes a cooktop and double sink with a polished chrome faucet. The custom cabinetry, made of fiddle-back anigre wood, extends up to the ceiling. The doors swing open to reveal a refrigerator, food pantry, small-appliance storage space and counters on which to use them, a microwave, and a dishwasher. There is even room in this behind-the-scenes area for the laundry equipment—a stacked washer and dryer. Contemporary styled lighting pendants suspended over the island provide ample task lighting. The cabinetry and the work areas visible when the doors are opened are illuminated with unobtrusive wall washer light fixtures.

whimsy in the kitchen

The renovation began with the removal of the existing low-loft ceiling and one dividing wall, and adding skylights to create an open space bathed in refreshing sunlight.

Located at one end of the entrance hall, the kitchen was reminiscent of the great halls in medieval castles.

A variety of materials, unusual shapes, and graphic themes create a fresh, vital atmosphere in this high-ceilinged English kitchen. In spite of its refined craftsmanship, it is designed to withstand daily use by the homeowners—a British rock star, his wife, and three children.

The home, originally built in the nineteenth century as a coach house and stables, had a charming sense of history that the owners wished to retain. But they also wanted it to be a fun, lively space. In the kitchen in particular, this became a challenge. The family hired a professional kitchen designer to turn the space into the kitchen of their dreams.

Traffic flows through clear passages on either side of a large island that combines a circular storage section and a tablelike attachment that includes a cooktop and drawers for cutlery.

The interests of the home-owners are reflected in the details. Their love of nature is illustrated in the hand-painted bands of fruit on the island.

Etched-glass panel designs are drawn from a circuit board, which reflects the owners' interest in technology.

The kitchen had to be an inviting place, since all who visited the home would enter there. Beyond the circular French doors at one end is a recording studio, and so the kitchen had to bear family traffic, be comfortable to cook in despite its narrow, 11-foot (3.35 m) width, and provide a place for working musicians to relax during breaks. A sense of order is achieved by organizing the kitchen into three areas: a cooking and food-preparation area in the center, a relaxation and dining area at one end, and the entrance hall at the other. Two of the sections provide counter workspace, but the heights between them vary to suit different tasks and heights of the users. The circular and angular shapes of the island are echoed in the shapes of the circular pot rack and rectangular ventilation hood suspended above it.

The two decorative themes developed for the kitchen—technology and nature—reflect the interests of the owners. The technology theme is reflected in the etched-glass circuit board patterning on the blue cupboard and in hand-painted motifs on the walls. The nature theme is expressed in a colorful, hand-painted band of fruits on the round portion of the island, in the stem-and-leaf shapes of the decorative ironwork in the loft area and on the dining table and chairs, and in the hand-painted birds circling the top of the tall cupboard.

The flooring includes an inlaid circle made with wedges of two types of limestone. The durable stone is positioned under the cooking and food-preparation areas, where timber would not have stood up well to heavy use. Woods used in the kitchen include cherry, sycamore, and aspen. The curving cabinetry and rounded shelving and cupboards reinforce the shape of the central circular island.

The dining and relaxation area is bathed in daylight and enhanced with a view to the garden terrace beyond by the large, Japanese-inspired, keyhole-shaped windows and door. The primary light fixtures are simple pendants suspended over work areas that complement the metalwork.

mixing woods & metal

The kitchen designer combined a variety of woods—including curly maple, mahogany, and redwood burl—to create this clean-lined yet visually interesting space.

It's all in the details. The stainless steel range and wall ovens serve as cool metal accents that set off the blend of warm woods.

The owners of this home wanted their 20-foot-by-17-foot (6.1 by 5.18 m) kitchen to look as modern as the rest of their home. The renovation of the kitchen also needed to add storage space, create an environment appropriate for casual entertaining, increase natural and electric light, and make the space more functional, yet flexible enough to accommodate more than one cook at a time.

A previously unused wall area is now used as a backdrop for a refrigerator, oven, and large pantry. The pantry gives the homeowners the increased storage capacity they craved, while increasing the efficiency of the space.

Attention to details has made this kitchen the unique space the homeowner requested. The countertops and backsplashes are made of durable Black Absolute granite, and the cabinet doors are inset with 3/8-inch (1 cm) -thick, sandblasted glass, both of which give the space a sense of depth and drama. An unusual finishing touch is the turned leg on the island that accents the eating bar area. The island is also enhanced by a striking curved piece of custom-molded glass textured with a sunburst pattern.

The owners' request for more daylight has been satisfied by replacing a small existing window with a large awning window, while a variety of lighting systems step in when the sun goes down. Lighting for countertop tasks comes from two sources: recessed downlights placed in front of the wall cabinets and fluorescent fixtures concealed beneath the wall cabinets. Pendant light fixtures are suspended over the island to provide task illumination and to add color to the room through their cobalt blue glass shades.

repeating color & pattern

The owner played a strong role in choosing materials, with some guidance from the designer. Attention to detail is evident in the use of color and materials.

To complement the cool blues, metal elements have been incorporated. The range hood, ovens, island sink, faucets, light fixtures, and refrigeration equipment are all made with stainless steel.

This homeowner dreamed of transforming her drab, confining, and poorly organized kitchen into the workspace of her dreams—functional and efficient, yet completely personalized with colors and materials she loved. While she felt she needed a professional's help, the owner—a professional agent who represents a variety of different artists—wanted to have a good deal of input on the overall design.

The goal for the kitchen designer was to use the owner's ideas and opinions to remodel the 23-foot-by-15-foot (7 by 4.6 m) kitchen into a contemporary styled space that blended cool blues and grays with warm cherry cabinetry and made the use of the limited space.

To make the room more efficient, a structural wall was removed to allow cabinets at the left of the sink to flow around the corner. The smaller island allows for wider aisles, which improves traffic flow through the space. Other improvements also increased efficiency while creating a less confined and more inviting space. The window area was enlarged, using three windows rather than one very large window, to create a framed view of the garden. The opening to the family room was also enlarged and framed with matching wood trim to create an interesting view.

The tall cabinets, ovens, and refrigeration equipment are grouped on the long wall opposite the windows, allowing the remainder of the room to appear larger and more open. The cooktop wall is 11 inches (27.9 cm) thick with a 6-inch (15.24 cm) -deep framed recess that creates the illusion of depth; both the hood and cooktop are visually contained within the frame. The range hood is designed with minimal bulk: it is only 9 inches (22.86 cm) high and offers display space, and the curved face allows vent coverage where needed above the cooktop.

Many hues of blue appear in the soapstone sink, the Blue Pearl granite countertops, the ceramic floor tiles that look like warm, old stones, and the multitextured fabric seat coverings. The backsplash is formed with rectangular blue glass tiles in glossy and matte finishes. These shades and textures all work together to create a complex harmony and maintain contemporary styling.

The natural cherry cabinets have Shaker-style doors. Matching cherry wood trims are used on the windows and doors. The owner did not want conventional cabinetry embellishments, but she had seen and loved cabinet designs inspired by Charles Rennie MacIntosh, the Scottish architect and Art Nouveau movement leader. And so, MacIntosh-inspired elements—primarily the grid patterns that characterized his work—have made their way into the room in several ways: a group of four squares is included at the top of each wall cabinet door, while a series of square copper accents is placed across the front of the range hood. Squares are also repeated on the corners of the matching cherry table.

bungalow beauty

Stainless steel diamond plate is used on the backsplash and a concrete shelf inset into it holds condiments.

When the owners of this 1930s California bungalow undertook an extensive renovation they added an entire wing, which allowed the kitchen to be relocated into what was formerly the dining room. The owners hired a professional to design a nontraditional, eclectic space with lots of unusual colors and materials.

The kitchen designer set out to create something special, beginning with the basic layout. The rectangular kitchen plan is set on a 6-degree angle. This allows extra-deep countertops to be included in certain areas to ease food preparation and a dropped soffit at right angles to the walls that enhances the angle of the cabinets. The layout also makes the kitchen seem more open than its modest 160 square feet.

The cabinets are made with a combination of two finishes: Italian walnut and black laminate. Several wall cabinet doors with glass inserts have been added to allow the owners to display china and glassware pieces collected during their frequent travels. Black laminate shelves frame the two main areas for cooking and cleanup and divide them from storage pantries and other appliances.

The concrete counter that overhangs the peninsula is inset with cast glass cut into diamond shapes.

Above the display cabinet to the left of the sink, a glass shelf—sunk directly into the studs—seems to float on the wall.

The unusual backsplash and kickplate under the countertop overhang are made with stainless steel diamond plate. The shiny metal contrasts with the matte cabinets and non-glossy, 3-inch (7.62 cm) -thick concrete countertops. A shallow concrete shelf inset into the backsplash is ideal for holding kitchen accessories.

Since the owners are both tall, they requested the countertops be installed 37 1/4 inches (94.62 cm), higher than the standard counter height, which is 36 inches (91 cm) from the finished floor. A special touch in the countertop that creates the seating overhang are the 3-inch (7.62 cm) -thick custom cast pieces of glass cut into diamond shapes and inset into the concrete. Because the glass is as thick as the countertop, the light shines through the glass to dapple the floor below. Concrete "legs" at either end of the sink connect with the concrete countertop and create a frame around the base cabinets.

Glass is used just as creatively elsewhere in the kitchen. Glass is used on top of the display cabinet, separating it visually as the display area. A frosted window to the right of the cooktop allows light to filter in from the southern exposure, while hiding a view of the neighbor's wall.

The kitchen is visually separated from the adjacent dining room by a dropped soffit painted pale sage green, and an angled column placed at the end of the cooktop. Glass shelves slice into the column for support and glow with the help of built-in lighting elements.

Open shelves set next to cabinets with inset glass doors helps the space seem larger and more open.

going retro

A sense of drama and elegance are added through the blending of interesting materials and textures.

The addition of a second sink makes it easy for two cooks to prepare and cook food at the same time.

The owners of this 104-square-foot kitchen are avid collectors of vintage objects and collectibles from the 1920s through the 1950s.

They hired kitchen designers to transform their lackluster, white laminate New York City apartment kitchen into a colorful, retro-looking space that would not only serve the practical purpose of increasing storage space, but serve as a fitting setting in which to display their collections.

The layout of the kitchen was not changed because budget and building requirements dictated that plumbing and gas lines remain in the original locations. But that's where the similarities between the old and new kitchens end.

The custom-designed cabinetry has aluminum doors fitted with circular bolts of metal hardware that add to the sleek look. Wall cabinet door fronts are inset with cobalt blue glass—a look reminiscent of the Art Deco period. The cabinet interiors are less expensive laminate-covered wood. So the look of all-metal cabinets is achieved without the more expensive price tag of all-metal cabinets.

The backsplash is made from one sheet of stainless steel so there are no seams to collect dirt and grime. The countertops and floor are made of Italian glass-chip terrazzo. The chips in the countertops are slightly larger than those in the floor tiles. This jazzy random-colored pattern adds a touch of the 1950s to the kitchen.

Packed into this city apartment kitchen are double wall ovens, a cooktop, a microwave, a dishwasher, and a stainless steel sink. There's a convenient wall-mounted eating bar opposite a brushed aluminum buffet. The buffet includes space for wine storage on either side. Storage space in the renovated kitchen was doubled when the cabinets were rebuilt all the way up to the ceiling.

The owners' collectibles have found homes on shelves above the dishwasher and eating bar. An added touch are a vintage stainless paper-towel holder and a silver-tone and black telephone mounted to the backsplash.

the fire in metal

Clean-lined mill-work and cherry wood cabinetry and a signature copper range hood distinguish the new kitchen.

This simple U-shape kitchen has taken on a sense of drama and elegance through the blending of interesting materials and textures. The designer used the influence of the ancient Oriental philosophies of feng shui to void the coldness and loss of energy that the main materials in the box-shaped kitchen would have inherited.

The most striking feature in this kitchen is the use of a firelike pattern in the metal panels used at the ends of the island and cabinet run, the range hood, and the frame around the oven. These elements have been set at a 10-degree angle to add further interest. The Oriental influence continues in the glass sashes in each corner, which are sandblasted with the pattern of a Japanese shoji screen. This pattern echoes the pattern of mullions in the adjacent audiovisual unit that is out of the range of the photo.

A versatile pivoting table adjacent to the island can be moved to face the television during casual meals or to be parallel to the island during a party. Cut in the same 10-degree, shark-fin shape it swings from a necessary structural pole that has attached to it storage baskets and light fixtures. A convenient niche for wine is built into the side of the island closest to the dining table. The large built-in refrigerator includes inset panels that allow it to blend in with adjacent cabinets. Rich Black Galaxy granite countertops and backsplashes match the black range and black trims on the clean-lined, contrasting light-colored cabinetry. The two sinks make it easy for two cooks to prepare and cook food at the same time.

Lighting fixtures concealed in the tops of the cabinetry cast uplight onto the white ceiling to give the room an uplifting feeling and make it seem larger. Unobtrusive recessed downlights provide the kitchen's general illumination. Decorative pendants offer task light above the island, while under-cabinet fixtures add light for performing tasks on the countertops. Lights inside the glass-door wall cabinets highlight china and other objects.

A wine cooler has been tucked into the end of the kitchen island. The opposite side has bins for holding reading materials.

penthouse phenomenon

The range is positioned in an interesting way with its large custom hood making a distinct design statement overhead.

Stainless steel sinks are set into concrete countertops.

The eating bar is made from board-formed concrete with the designer's signature purple coloration.

Adding light to the space is a bank of existing windows and angled skylights that are part of the renovation.

This kitchen, owned by a San Francisco developer and his family, is part of a penthouse apartment. The wood used for the custom cabinetry is an unusual bleached anigre. The designer offset its warm, light hue with concrete countertops and heavy-duty, stainless steel appliances.

A wealth of custom elements contributes to the kitchen's innovative look. The flooring is a combination of acid-etched concrete poured in place with integral color and cherry wood. The walls are given character with paint and veneer plaster.

The range hood, made of stainless steel and plaster, represents an earthy element symbolically descending from the sky into the hearth of the home. Next to the range, a bank of perforated stainless steel shelves are concealed behind ribbed-glass doors.

The roof, originally flat, has been reconfigured to look like a shifting plane.

The countertop is a unique combination of stainless and wood.

KITCHEN WORKBOOK

EVERYTHING YOU NEED TO PLAN YOUR NEW KITCHEN, INCLUDING:

BUDGET-PLANNER CHECKLIST • TAKING MEASUREMENTS • KITCHEN RENOVATION CALENDAR • DESIGNING YOUR SPACE • CABINETS AND COUNTERTOPS • LIGHTING • COLOR

planning your renovation

Properly planning a new kitchen is as important as choosing the right materials and installing them precisely. Don't start falling in love with any materials or appliances until you've estimated your entire budget and carefully measured your space. Consider hiring a professional designer to help you during this very important phase—he or she will have insights into how best to use your space, tips for creating a functional and beautiful area, and ideas for stretching your budget as far as it will go. An experienced contractor will see problems and potential much more quickly than a first-time do-it-yourselfer, and will offer solutions that might not come to the homeowner until the renovation is well underway, or even completed.

THE BUDGET

According to the National Kitchen and Bath Association, the average kitchen renovation costs from $15,000 to $26,000, including design, products, and installation, although some renovations can come in for much less, and of course, others can run much, much higher. You can shave off some of the costs by doing much of the work yourself, but remember that some jobs—including electrical and plumbing work—are best left to professionals.

Cabinetry will eat up about half of your total budget. Prices are affected by materials (oak is more expensive than pine, for example), quality of the product, whether you use stock cabinets or have them custom made, and whether you have them professionally installed. Costs for countertops and backsplashes will also change based on these factors.

Like cabinetry, the price of your floors will be decided on what you choose and how you install it. Many floors, especially the new European laminate flooring so popular in kitchens today, are easy for the do-it-yourselfer to install in a weekend; others, like ceramic tile, are probably best left to a professional.

There are a few areas where a bit of elbow grease can save a great deal of money. Handle any and all demolition on your own; tear out the old cabinets, floors, drywall, and anything else you plan to replace, borrowing or renting a truck to drag it all off to the dump at the end of the day. If you're good at installing drywall, by all means take on that project yourself, along with any wallpapering, plastering, or painting.

TIMING

When planning your renovation, think not only about money but about time. A project being handled entirely by professionals, in a vacant house, can be done in a few weeks, but only if all the materials you need are readily available and your time frame works for all the professionals you hire. A do-it-yourself project, handled mainly on weekends, can drag on for months. If you plan ahead, ordering all the materials, appliances, and cabinetry long before you begin the demolition, the renovation work itself can be handled quickly, with the kitchen out of commission for the least amount of time.

EXPECT THE UNEXPECTED

Tackling a kitchen renovation is not for the faint of heart. Be prepared for costs that almost always go beyond the estimated: unexpected costs—from requiring new plumbing or wiring when you thought the old system would hold up, to suddenly deciding that you simply must have that top-of-the-line cooktop from France—are the Murphy's Law of home renovation. And the first corollary to that law is that your kitchen renovation will always take longer than you expected. Despite painstaking planning, there will be delays in the arrival of materials, of contractors or subcontractors, or just days when you need to get out and do something other than work on your kitchen.

Similarly, everyone in the house must be prepared to live with weeks, possibly months of dust, noise, and limited kitchen facilities. Weeks may go by when you don't have a kitchen sink, months without an oven. To save your sanity, consider creating a "mini-kitchen" in an extra bathroom or laundry room: borrow or rent a minifridge (or move the old one to someplace accessible), and set up a table with a microwave oven, toaster oven, coffee pot, and electric tea kettle. Have a stack of take-out menus handy and plenty of paper plates and plasticware, and remember that when it's all over, you'll have that kitchen of your dreams.

budget-planner checklist

demolition

Do-it-yourself or hire a pro?

Budget $ ________________

plumbing

Do-it-yourself or hire a pro?

Plumber name/number ____

Wish list ____

____

____

____

____

Budget $ ________________

electrical

Do-it-yourself or hire a pro?

Electrician name/number ____

Wish list ____

____

____

____

____

Budget $ ________________

carpentry

Do-it-yourself or hire a pro?

Carpenter name/number ____

What's required (moving/rebuilding walls) ______________________________

____

____

____

____

Budget $ ________________

cabinetry and countertops

Do-it-yourself or hire a pro?

Cabinetmaker name/number ______________________

Cabinets ______________________

Counters ______________________

Options ______________________

____

____

____

____

Budget $ __________

appliances

Refrigerator ______________________ $ __________

Oven/range ______________________ $ __________

Dishwasher ______________________ $ __________

Trash compactor ______________________ $ __________

Microwave ______________________ $ __________

Exhaust system ______________________ $ __________

floor

Do-it-yourself or hire a pro?

Type of floor and cost ______________________

______________________ $ __________

total budget

$ __________

measuring up

You might be dreaming of colors, textures, appliances, and lighting, but when it comes to planning a kitchen renovation, there is one definitive starting point: an accurate and complete measurement of your space. Before you can design a floor plan, you must determine the size of the room, note the locations and sizes of doors and windows, and factor in existing plumbing and electrical. Lay it all out on graph paper, and begin playing with different layouts to determine if you need to make any adjustments to the basic foundation of the room. Remember, every wall you decide to knock out or move, every window that you determine is too big or too small, and each additional light socket, electrical outlet, and plumbing line will drastically affect your budget and your timetable.

Measuring might sound like a fairly simple and straightforward procedure, but getting accurate measurements takes more than a few minutes and a cloth tape measure.

Tips for Measuring Your Kitchen

- Use a retractable metal tape measure for curved spaces and short measures.
- Use a folding carpenter's ruler to measure longer distances such as walls and ceilings, where a tape measure might sag and render a skewed measure.
- Use graph paper to create an outline of the room, and mark each measure appropriately—include the lengths of the walls, size and location of windows, doorways, and closets. You can draw it to scale or do a "rough" outline for now, and do a scale version when you're finished.
- Use a pencil—that eraser will come in handy.
- Calculate all measures to within 1/8 (.3 cm) of an inch.
- Always measure twice! If you get two different readings, measure again, and again, until you're certain that you've got it right.
- Take more than one floor-to-ceiling reading for each wall, since few homes have perfectly level floors and ceilings.
- Take all horizontal measures at counter height.
- Include space you'll be adding—closets you are knocking out, for example, in your diagram.
- Calculate the length and width of each window and doorway, as well as its location on the wall—how far from the floor, how far from the ceiling, how far from the corners of the room, how far from one another.
- Include all trim in your measures for doors and windows.
- Incorporate swing space—the space required for the door to open into or out of the kitchen—for all doorways.
- For open kitchens, create a phantom wall in your diagram to denote the borderline of the space. Measure the borderline carefully, and note the location of important features beyond it: views you don't want to block, etc.
- Keep all your measurements in one place—they'll come in handy at every phase, from buying appliances to choosing kitchen curtains.

MEASUREMENT RECORD

Item/Space	Dimensions
Walls	
Wall One length	
Wall Two length	
Wall Three length	
Wall Four length	
Wall Five length	
Wall Six length	
Wall One height	
Wall Two height	
Wall Three height	
Wall Four height	
Wall Five height	
Wall Six height	
Doorway One	
Distance from corner A	
Distance from corner B	
Height and width (include trim)	
Swing space for door	
Doorway Two	
Distance from corner A	
Distance from corner B	
Height and width (include trim)	
Swing space for door	
Doorway Three	
Distance from corner A	
Distance from corner B	
Height and width (include trim)	
Swing space for door	
Window One	
Height and width (include trim)	
Distance from corner A	
Distance from corner B	
Distance from floor	

Item/Space	Dimensions
Window Two	
Height and width (include trim)	
Distance from corner A	
Distance from corner B	
Distance from floor	
Window Three	
Height and width (include trim)	
Distance from corner A	
Distance from corner B	
Distance from floor	
Window Four	
Height and width (include trim)	
Distance from corner A	
Distance from corner B	
Distance from floor	
Window Five	
Height and width (include trim)	
Distance from corner A	
Distance from corner B	
Distance from floor	
Pantry	
Wall One	
Wall Two	
Wall Three	
Wall Four	
Doorway	
Wall height	
Architectural features	
Fireplaces, stairways, etc.	

Other helpful things to note

Keep the locations of existing electrical and plumbing on hand to make planning even easier.

Item	Location
Water line (for sink and/or dishwasher)	
Additional water line	
Drain pipes	
Gas lines	
Heat vents	
Electrical outlets	
Overhead electrical	
Heat sources: Floor vents,	
radiators, baseboards, etc.	

timing

As we've mentioned, and as everyone who's ever tackled a renovation will tell you, scheduling is almost as important as budget. Every decision you make will affect the overall schedule for your renovation. If you are considering taking on a kitchen renovation as a do-it-yourselfer, be prepared to have the project stretched out over many weeks or even months, and kiss your weekends and vacation time good-bye. But even if you decide to bring in a contractor, there are countless variables that can slow down the project—from bad weather that prevents windows from being replaced, to other clients whose projects run over and push yours back.

Depending on the extent of your renovation, the project might take a matter of weeks or it may stretch out over several months. A well-thought-out timetable will help you to put the project into perspective and keep it on track. Remember, your decisions will affect the schedule: You might be able to pick up ready-made cabinets at a home store tomorrow, or you might choose custom cabinets that will take a craftsman many months to complete. With these factors in mind, you can break down your schedule into phases. Each phase might account for a week for a quickie makeover, or a month for a carefully planned out and executed renovation.

KITCHEN RENOVATION CALENDAR

phase one: planning

From __________ to __________

- [ ] determine extent of renovation
- [ ] determine a budget
- [ ] acquire financing (loan, mortgage, savings, etc.)
- [ ] settle on a time frame
- [ ] hire an architect
- [ ] hire a plumber
- [ ] hire an electrician
- [ ] hire a carpenter
- [ ] hire an interior or kitchen designer

____

____

____

____

____

____

phase two: demolition

From __________ to __________

- [ ] Do-it-yourself or hire demolition team
- [ ] Check on refuse rules (if doing it yourself)
- [ ] Call carting service

____

____

____

____

____

____

phase three: design

From __________ to __________

- determine how many/what kinds of appliances
- determine number of workstations
- consider construction of space, moving walls, etc.
- decide on a layout

____

____

____

____

____

____

phase four: shopping

From __________ to __________

- appliances
- lighting fixtures
- plumbing fixtures
- cabinetry
- flooring
- décor
- other details

____

____

____

____

____

____

Tips for Every Phase

PHASE ONE: PLANNING

Factor things like budgeting into your schedule—will you need to get a homeowner's loan? Or will you have to save some money? Don't forget to think about overall timing. When's the best time to start? When the kids go back to college? Or during the summer, when you have some vacation time to tackle things yourself?

PHASE TWO: DESIGN

Creating the perfect layout can be simple or incredibly complex. You might budget in just a weekend for this phase, taking your own measurements of the space and having your local home design store come up with a few options. Or you might hire an architect and designer to come in, assess the space, and return to you several weeks later with a few different plans. Whichever option you use, be sure you have properly identified all your needs—number of workstations, priorities for appliances, and the like—before you finalize your design.

PHASE THREE: SHOPPING

Finding the perfect fixtures—from the six-burner cooktop right down to the knobs on the bread drawer—can be a fun and frustrating experience. But it's imperative that you do a good deal of your shopping long before you hire anyone to start working on your kitchen. After all, you don't want to tear out your old kitchen only to find that the refrigerator you want won't be available for two or three months. By having all your decisions straight before work begins, your kitchen will only be out of commission for the minimum amount of time—and you'll be able to ensure that the tile backsplash doesn't clash with the tile floor!

PHASE FOUR: DEMOLITION

This is a project that most homeowners can take on in a weekend. Find out about sanitation regulations in your area: you may have to hire a private carting service to remove the debris and your old appliances may have to be recycled.

phase five: electrical and plumbing

From __________ to __________

- [ ] determine needs
- [ ] get estimates
- [ ] check references
- [ ] install new electric
- [ ] install new plumbing
- [ ] repair or replace heating units
- [ ] repair or replace ventilation units

phase six: walls and foundations

From __________ to __________

- [ ] install drywall on walls and ceilings
- [ ] finish taping and sanding
- [ ] prime walls for paint
- [ ] replace or repair subfloor

phase seven: floors

From __________ to __________

- [ ] order materials ahead of time
- [ ] install floor, or hire flooring specialist
- [ ] determine set time for new floor

phase eight: cabinet installation and other carpentry

From __________ to __________

- [ ] order cabinets early
- [ ] check in regularly with carpenter to maintain schedule

phase nine: paint/ wallpaper/finishwork

From __________ to __________

- [ ] order wallpaper and purchase paint early
- [ ] hire professionals or purchase tools to do-it-yourself

____

____

____

____

____

____

phase ten: appliance installation

From __________ to __________

- [ ] order early
- [ ] confirm dates for delivery
- [ ] call for delivery when ready

____

____

____

____

____

____

Tips for Every Phase

PHASE FIVE: ELECTRICAL AND PLUMBING

Make sure each professional is licensed and stands behind his work, and check all references: ask not only about the quality of the work but the timeliness with which it was completed.

PHASE SIX: WALLS AND FOUNDATIONS

Getting the drywall installed and finished is one of the messiest and most frustrating parts of any construction project. It can't be begun until after the electrical and plumbing work is finished, and it takes several days to complete.

PHASE SEVEN: FLOORS

A floating wood or laminate floor can go down in a day; a tile floor will take several days. Be sure to determine how long you'll need to stay off the floor after it's put down, as that will affect the rest of your schedule.

PHASE EIGHT: CABINET INSTALLATION AND OTHER CARPENTRY

If you've shopped and ordered early, or if you bought ready-made, you should be able to get the cabinets installed in a day or two.

PHASE NINE: PAINT/WALLPAPER/FINISHWORK

Depending on the extent of the work, this can take anywhere from a day to a few days if you're having custom moldings installed.

PHASE TEN: APPLIANCE INSTALLATION

If you've ordered early and have them ready when you need them, they can go relatively quickly.

designing your space

Whether you're planning to hire a professional designer or you're tackling the project yourself, creating the perfect layout for your kitchen is one of the biggest challenges to any renovation. Finding the best way to use your space depends not only on creative thinking but also on familiarity with the essential rules and terms of kitchen design. After all, a creative and interesting design is worthless if it's not entirely functional, and adhering to the basic rules regarding will insure that it is. A few things to keep in mind:

- Make sure that nothing obstructs the flow of traffic within the work triangle.
- Incorporate swing space into your layout—remember, you dishwasher may only be 21 inches (53 cm) deep, but you'll need a few feet of open space in front of it to open the door and use it
- When you're designing your cabinetry, the key word is frontage—the width of the front of all your units combined.
- You'll need at least 125 inches (318 cm) of frontage for a smaller kitchen (say, less than 150 square feet); larger rooms can afford more.
- Countertops should be 36 inches (91 cm) high. You can install a few sections at higher or lower levels to suit tall short or tall cooks, but keep most of the counters at standard height.
- Don't tuck your oven or dishwasher into a corner . . . you'll need a bit of space on both sides of the open door to access things on the counters.
- Think about whether you'll want a single-, double-, or even triple-basin sink before your decide on a layout . . . the number of basins will affect the sink's overall size.

Standards for kitchen design

ITEM	STANDARD DIMENSIONS
Work triangle	No more than 26 feet (7.92 m) total perimeter; each leg at least 4 feet (1.2 m) but no more than or longer than 9 feet (2.7 m)
Doorway width	At least 32 inches (81 cm)
Work aisles	At least 42 inches (107 cm) wide
Prep space	At least 36 inches (81 cm) of countertop, near the main sink
Wall cabinets	12 inches (30 cm) deep; at least 30 inches (76 cm) tall
Base cabinets	21 inches (53 cm) deep; 36 inches (91 cm) tall
Countertops	21 inches (53 cm) deep; 36 inches (91 cm) high
Clearance below wall cabinets	15 to 18 inches (38 cm to 46 cm)
Refrigerator	16 cubic feet of refrigerator space for the first two family members and add another 1.5 cubic feet for each additional member.

WORKSHEET: APPLIANCE FACTS

There are so many different styles and sizes available for appliances today that it's easy to come home after a day of shopping having forgotten everything you've seen. Use this chart to keep track of the different models—having specifications for a few different models will come in handy when you're building your layout.

Item	Choice A	Choice B
Sink	Brand ______	Brand ______
	No. of basins ______	No. of basins ______
	Finish ______	Finish ______
	Disposal ______	Disposal ______
	Other features ______	Other features ______
	______	______
	Dimensions ______	Dimensions ______
Faucet	Brand ______	Brand ______
	Finish ______	Finish ______
	Built-in sprayer ______	Built-in sprayer ______
	Built-in filter ______	Built-in filter ______
	Other features ______	Other features ______
	______	______
Range	Brand ______	Brand ______
	Finish ______	Finish ______
	Gas or electric ______	Gas or electric ______
	Btus ______	Btus ______
	Features ______	Features ______
	______	______
	Dimensions ______	Dimensions ______

Item	Choice A	Choice B
Oven	Brand ____________	Brand ____________
	Finish ____________	Finish ____________
	Wall or freestanding ____________	Wall or freestanding ____________
	Gas or electric ____________	Gas or electric ____________
	Btus ____________	Btus ____________
	Features ____________	Features ____________
	____________	____________
	Dimensions ____________	Dimensions ____________
Microwave	Brand ____________	Brand ____________
	Finish ____________	Finish ____________
	Built-in or freestanding ____________	Built-in or freestanding ____________
	Power ____________	Power ____________
	Features ____________	Features ____________
	____________	____________
	Dimensions ____________	Dimensions ____________
Refrigerator	Brand ____________	Brand ____________
	Finish ____________	Finish ____________
	Configuration ____________	Configuration ____________
	Cubic feet ____________	Cubic feet ____________
	Energy rating ____________	Energy rating ____________
	Ice/Water ____________	Ice/Water ____________
	Other features ____________	Other features ____________
	____________	____________
	Dimensions ____________	Dimensions ____________

Item	Choice A	Choice B
Dishwasher	Brand __________	Brand __________
	Finish __________	Finish __________
	Features __________	Features __________
	Dimensions __________	Dimensions __________
Other Appliances		

cabinets and countertops

The typical American kitchen is defined by cabinetry: the configuration of the units creates the workstations and determines the traffic flow, the features of the units introduce functionality and storage, and the style of the cabinets sets the tone for the entire kitchen. It's no wonder, then, that in most kitchen renovations, cabinetry eats up about 50 percent of the total budget. So it's important to choose your cabinets carefully, whether you are using them to create a simple galley-style layout or an elaborate live-in kitchen complete with a huge island for both preparing and enjoying meals.

When it comes to cabinetry and countertops, you must consider both form and function. Your units must be durable, as they will be open, closed, slammed, leaned upon, soiled, cleaned, and resoiled several times each day. Fortunately, some of the industry's most popular and attractive materials are also the most durable. Solid oak, maple, and cherry remain the most popular woods for cabinets, and butcherblock, tile, and laminate make beautiful and functional countertops. More modern finishes, such as stainless steel and solid surfacing, are also attractive and sensible choices.

Remember that the look of your cabinets doesn't end with the cabinets: to achieve a real built-in look, you'll need to install a toekick beneath the base cabinets, which also prevents errant crumbs from wandering out of sweeping range and attracting pests. Think also about how your wall cabinets will meet the ceiling. Some cooks prefer to leave the space above empty, perhaps finishing the cabinets off with dential or other decorative moulding, or using the space as a display and storage area for breadbaskets, cookbooks, or cumbersome platters and trays. For a more permanent, custom look, you might have your carpenter create a fascia and soffit above the cabinets, and install crown molding where they meet.

Kitchen Extras

Of course, not all cabinetry need be built-in. Freestanding units—be they new or antique—add a touch of unexpected yet contemporary charm to the kitchen. Put pots and pans within easy reach and allow cooks to show off their prized batterie of cookware. Other simple additions—from open shelving to wall storage systems—can add character and functionality to your cooking space.

- Add an antique armoire or buffet to store serving pieces, linens, even small appliances in style.
- A baker's rack was born for the kitchen and adds a touch of contemporary charm.
- Suspending pots and pans from the ceiling frees up cabinet space and keeps them all within reach.
- Adorn a bare wall with a metal grid fitted with simple hooks to store utensils and kitchen gadgets right where you need them.
- Simple rod systems—which can be outfitted with anything from cup hooks to paper towel holders to wine racks—are available for installation beneath wall cabinets.
- Don't forget about a spice rack.
- Narrow open shelves allow gourmets to display prized vinegars, oils, seasonings, cooking wines, and other ingredients.
- Medical supply cabinets—stripped down to the bare steel or repainted in autobody shops—add versatile and clean looking storage.

CABINETRY WORKSHEET

style of cabinets

- ☐ Custom
- ☐ Stock
- ☐ Semicustom

finish

- ☐ Natural wood finish
- ☐ Laminate
- ☐ Steel or other metal
- ☐ Painted wood
- ☐ Other ______________________________

unit style

- ☐ Framed
- ☐ Frameless

door styles

- ☐ Contemporary
- ☐ Traditional
- ☐ Country
- ☐ Wood panel
- ☐ Glass panel
- ☐ Other ______________________________
- ☐ Mix of ______________________________

decorative features

- ☐ Crown moldings
- ☐ Dential or other moldings
- ☐ Soffit/fascia, or open to ceiling

hardware

- Hinges: concealed or decorative ______________________
- Knobs and pulls ________________________________

functional storage

- Slide-out shelving
- Functionally designed drawers for silverware, utensils, spices, bread, even pots and pans
- Corner cabinet with a built-in lazy Susan
- Built-in plate rack for storing and displaying your dishes.
- Countertop "garage" for small appliances
- Built-in, slide-out cutting boards
- Built-in bins for storing root vegetables and fruit
- Built-in knife rack
- Rolling larder to hold drygoods
- Sponge bin in front of sink
- Slide-out, dual trash cans tucked beneath base cabinets
- Cookbook storage
- Microwave storage
- Shelving for frequently used or display items
- Hanging pot racks
- Message center
- Countertop sections of butcherblock for food prep, and/or marble for pastry
- Swing-out storage for heavy small appliances (stand-up mixers or food processors)

countertops

- [ ] Butcherblock
- [ ] Stainless steel
- [ ] Stone
- [ ] Marble
- [ ] Tile
- [ ] Laminate
- [ ] Solid surfacing (Corian or other ________________________)
- [ ] Mix of ____
- [ ] Other ____

backsplash

- [ ] Tile
- [ ] Countertop surface
- [ ] Other ____

special treatments

- [ ] Work island
- [ ] Dining bar
- [ ] Computer station
- [ ] Bookshelves

lighting

Any designer or stylist will tell you that even the most beautiful design jobs can be disasters if they are improperly lit. This truism is even more apropos in a multifunctional room like the kitchen, where food is both prepared and eaten, and where families and friends gather. So it's important to devise a lighting concept for your kitchen, and—since kitchen lights are usually built in, and thus require electrical work—it's extremely important to create your lighting scheme during the planning stages, before you hire an electrician.

The first kind of lighting you should consider is natural light—the light that streams in through your windows and fills the room. Your design should always take natural light into consideration; indeed, in a home renovation or building project, it would be wise to place the kitchen at the end of the house that gets the most morning or afternoon light. Within the room, windows should be installed to capture as much light as possible, and placing your main work area or your sink in front of a window with lots of light and a pretty view can make your time spend there even more pleasant. Since natural light changes throughout the day and can be further enhanced (or dimmed) with window treatments, it is almost a living aspect of your design.

The second form of lighting you'll need to think about is general lighting. Very few kitchens can function without a primary light source or two that illuminates the entire room. For most kitchens, this means a ceiling light, and the choices for the fixture are endless. You might consider a simple florescent kitchen light, which provides good lighting and saves on energy costs. Or perhaps you are more interested in recessed lights that disappear into the ceiling for a more modern look. Or look for an attractive hanging fixture that enhances and complements the décor of the room. A multifunctional illuminated ceiling fan that both lights the room and improves air circulation can be a great addition. Whatever kind of fixture you choose, be sure to locate switches close to doorways, so that they can be easily found in the dark.

The third form of lighting that you must consider in a kitchen is task lighting. After all, you'll be wielding knives, inspecting meat, and washing vegetables in this room—you need to really see what you're doing. A simple and unobtrusive solution is to install simple fluorescents beneath the wall cabinets: they'll illuminate the work surfaces below without becoming too hot or producing a harsh glare. You'll need to add task lighting to each work area, so consider using different fixtures for different spots.

A fourth type of lighting to consider is accent lighting. Adding a night light or a dimmer switch on your main fixture can create a soft glow in the wee hours and provide a safe, clear path for midnight snackers. Creative use of low-wattage lamps—be they elegant wall sconces or simple paper-shaded Chinese-style lanterns—can add an attractive touch of accent lighting when your kitchen's not in regular use.

LIGHTING WORKSHEET

general lighting

Number of fixtures ______________________

Electric hookups ready? ______________________

Style of fixtures

- [ ] Recessed
- [ ] Pendant or hanging
- [ ] Track
- [ ] Downlights (cans)
- [ ] Sconces
- [ ] Undercabinet fixtures
- [ ] Overcabinet fixtures
- [ ] Ceiling fan
- [ ] Other ______________________
- [ ] Total number of bulbs per fixture ______________

Type of light

- [ ] Fluorescent
- [ ] Incandescent
- [ ] Halogen
- [ ] Other ______________________

task lighting

Work Area 1

____

Electric hookups ready? ______________________

Style of fixture ______________________

Type of light

- [ ] Fluorescent
- [ ] Incandescent
- [ ] Halogen
- [ ] Other ______________________

Work Area 2

____

Electric hookups ready? ______________________________

Style of fixture ______________________________

Type of light

☐ Fluorescent

☐ Incandescent

☐ Halogen

☐ Other ______________________________

Work Area 3

____

Electric hookups ready? ______________________________

Style of fixture ______________________________

Type of light

☐ Fluorescent

☐ Incandescent

☐ Halogen

☐ Other ______________________________

accent lighting

Light Source 1

____

Electric hookups ready? ______________________________

Type of fixture

☐ Wall sconces

☐ Night-light

☐ Table lamp

☐ Other ______________________________

Dimmer switches

Number of switches ______________________________

For which fixtures ______________________________

Type of light

☐ Fluorescent

☐ Incandescent

☐ Halogen

☐ Other ______________________________

Light Source 2

____

Electric hookups ready? ______________

Type of fixture

- [ ] Wall sconces
- [ ] Night-light
- [ ] Table lamp
- [ ] Other ______________

Dimmer switches

Number of switches ______________

For which fixtures ______________

Type of light

- [ ] Fluorescent
- [ ] Incandescent
- [ ] Halogen
- [ ] Other ______________

Light Source 3

____

Electric hookups ready? ______________

Type of fixture

- [ ] Wall sconces
- [ ] Night-light
- [ ] Table lamp
- [ ] Other ______________

Dimmer switches

Number of switches ______________

For which fixtures ______________

Type of light

- [ ] Fluorescent
- [ ] Incandescent
- [ ] Halogen
- [ ] Other ______________

color

The colors you choose reflect your style and your sense, and can be the most satisfying and personal aspect of kitchen design. But it's important to be careful with color, too. Countertops and cabinets are long-term investments, and will likely be around longer than any trendy color will be in style: Think of the avocado green countertops of the 1970s, and the chiffon-pink appliances of the 1950s.

But painted surfaces, window treatments, linens, and floors can be changed with relative ease and often at little expense. So, while your conservative superego might be opting for sensible stainless steel appliances and stark white countertops, you can indulge your id with bright red walls, whimsical painted cabinetry, or a vibrant floral-patterned linoleum floor.

Presently, the most popular colors are rich hues that evoke exotic locales or natural elements, as well as vibrant nostalgic shades reminiscent of Depression-era glass. Deep, spicy shades of saffron and cinnamon, or pale, cool shades of blue and green are popular in the kitchen, and all trends indicate that they will continue to turn up in the kitchen.

But your kitchen colors should reflect more than just the trends of the day. Use them to express your spirit, your style, and your culinary inspirations. A chef specializing in Asian cuisine might be inspired by a kitchen decked out in deep black appliances with splashes of red; a Mediterranean cook might take her inspiration from a yellow, blue, and green platter purchased during a trip to Tuscany. A kitchen might take its color from the white and blue buildings of the Greek Isles, or from the misty green fields of the Irish countryside.

And remember, color is more than just paint: earthy terra-cotta tiles, collectible Fire King dinnerware, tinted glass, brightly patterned curtains, and color-stained woods combine to offer a bevy of ways to introduce, accent, or complement colors in your kitchen.

Adding Splashes of Color

- Paint the insides of open cabinetry in a color that contrasts and complements the exterior.
- Paint, pickle, or stain your hardwood floors in a color that pleases you.
- Display collectibles that complement your color scheme.
- Paint each wall a different, complementary color to create huge planes of color.
- Add privacy and a bolt of color with richly hued window treatments.
- Tile a backsplash with attractive art tiles, either in all one color, or in a vibrant mix of shades.
- Don't underestimate the value of white: use it as an accent against pale or dark colored walls.

HOT PALETTES

Think of the spicy shades of a Marrakesh market: Rich, vibrant reds, and full, warm yellows, paired with peppery blacks and sun-bleached desert sand. Exotic colors in the kitchen are only natural in an age when food, décor, and eating all reflect a new global culture. You could work with one or more shades, and pair them with natural substances like wood and stone, as well as with man-made furnishings of wrought iron, steel, or glass.

WATER PALETTES

According to color theorists, blue is an appetite suppressant, making it a questionable choice for the kitchen: after all, very few natural foods are blue! But the color is incredibly popular in kitchens ranging from high-end industrial-style spaces to homey, country styled spaces. It works for a number of reasons. First of all, blue is a natural color for creating a calm, soothing atmosphere, a welcome feature in what can often be the most hectic room in the house. And blues can open a room up: walls or ceilings painted even dark shades of blue appear to recede, a definite plus in a small space. Perhaps most important, blue is a wonderful foil for other colors: it is a perfect foil for bright, sunny yellows, and makes whites appear cleaner and fresher.

NEUTRAL PALETTES

Perhaps your dream of color is a rainbow of soft, calming neutrals. Avoiding vibrant or bright colors does not mean your scheme must be dull. Combine soft, creamy shades of ivory with pale pinks, blues, and greens to create a soothing yet far from boring space, and to keep the focus on your furnishings—and your food.

EARTHY PALETTES

Envision a rich terra-cotta floor, paired with plaster walls glazed in a warm shade of yellow. Rooms that evoke the colors and textures of the earth attract us on a most primal level, and with good reason: all of our food comes from the earth and a much of our food comes in earthy colors. By sticking to rich, earthy hues, you'll be reinforcing the warm, welcoming aspects of your kitchen.

GARDEN PALETTES

Of course, the earth also produces lots of leaves, grass, and herbs, and a color scheme based on green can be immensely satisfying. Color theorists cite green as an uplifting and life-affirming color, and with a palette ranging from palest pistachio to rich bottle or hunter green, there's a green that will work with every style and every sensibility. And just as in the garden, colors ranging from morning glory blue to American Beauty red look striking when paired with the perfect shade of green.

ACHROMATIC PALETTES

As modern and fresh today as it was when it first gained popularity in the 1930s, the black-and-white palette remains a classic of kitchen design. The stark contrast between the two colorless colors provides a fresh, clean look that works as well on kitchen floors as it does on chef's pants. And it works equally well in a purely black-and-white format as it does when accented with splashes of bright, vivid color or pale, soft pastels.

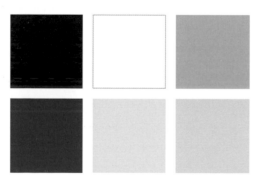

NOTES

* Raised ledge on dividing counter bet kit & dining room can be a good place for guests to hang; homework etc. See p17.
- I like window under cabinet look p77.
- Check out marble vs. granite countertops.
- I like the suspension system and work zone ideas on p83.
- Try to put stuff in the island - microwave, etc. Place island at an angle?
- Countertop in baking area can be lower to make work easier.
- Recycling center under/near sink
- I like the color scheme on pp108-109. Door handles too
- Range hood copper or st. steele w/copper inset.
- Use frosted glass in all new rooms to allow light & maintain privacy.

* It's important that we have a place for people to congregate in the kitchen separated from the cooks space & traffic area.

KITCHEN RESOURCES

Use this guide for gathering information on design, products, planning, and professional services. The designers and manufacturers listed are those who have contributed to this book.

DESIGN & PLANNING INFORMATION

American Institute of Architects (AIA)
www.aia.org

Details on what architects are qualified to do, as well as a locator service are included.

Ameican Society of Interior Designers (ASID)
www.asid.org

Advice on design and on how to choose an interior designer, as well as a locator feature.

HomePortfolio
www.homeportfolio.com

Information on products and advice on many aspects of home design.

Homestore
www.homestore.com

Home improvement information of all kinds, including do-it-yourself remodeling projects and home buying services.

ImproveNet
www.improvenet.com

Information on lenders and home repairs, with assistance in finding professional help from contractors to architects.

Kitchen-Bath.com
www.kitchen-bath.com

This informational site is for homeowners, though it is produced by Kitchen & Bath Business, the leading magazine for kitchen and bath industry professionals. Useful, easy-to-read articles cover products, installation techniques, and design advice.

Kitchens.com
www.kitchens.com

A designer locator is featured, along with information on products, the building process, and planning.

National Kitchen & Bath Association (NKBA)
www.nkba.org

The site offers you the chance to receive a kitchen and bath workbook, along with information on professional help in your area and tips on good kitchen planning. The NKBA is the association for kitchen and bath dealers and design specialists, and offers programs that qualify professionals as Certified Kitchen Designers.

RETAILERS

bulthaup corporation (on cover)
The Prince Building, 306
578, Broadway
New York, NY 10012
212-966-7183
fax: 212-966-0790

California Closets

800-873-4264
www.californiaclosets.com

Customized, built-in systems for storage.

Crate & Barrel
888-249-4158
www.crateandbarrel.com

Household accessories, cooking supplies, and decorative place settings.

Decoratetoday.com
800-575-8016
www.decoratetoday.com

An extensive selection of wallpaper, blinds, custom-framed art, rugs, lighting, and home accents. Orders taken online.

Expo Design Center
www.homedepot.com

A more upscale version of and sister company to Home Depot, these centers offer remodeling and design services as well as an extensive range of products, many displayed in up-to-date vignettes that reflect current design trends. Information on Expo locations can be obtained through the Home Depot Web site.

Hold Everything
800-421-2264
www.holdeverything.com

Storage options and accessories.

Home Depot
www.homedepot.com

An extensive selection of kitchen, bath, and other home products as well as professionals on staff who can help with design and remodeling planning. The site includes a retail store locator. Online purchasing is also available in some cities.

Ikea
800-434-4532 to place orders and for store locations
410-931-8940 East Coast
818-912-1199 West Coast
www.ikea-usa.com

Furniture, storage options, and accessories priced affordably.

Kitchenetc.com
800-232-4070
www.kitchenetc.com

Online-only shop offering china and tabletop items, cookbooks, and bakeware.

Klaff's
800-KLAFFS-1
www.klaffs.com

This upscale home design center is Connecticut based, with locations in South Norwalk, Westport, and Danbury. Kitchen, bath, decorative hardware, lighting, and accessories lines are carried and design services are available.

The Great Indoors
303-708-2500
www.thegreatindoors.com

This home center features the full gamut of products for kitchen, bath, and bedroom, along with design and installation services.

Williams-Sonoma
800-840-2591
www.williams-sonoma.com

Small kitchen appliances, utensils, gourmet food items, and other kitchen accessories.

PRODUCT MANUFACTURERS

ABBAKA
1500-A Burke Avenue
San Francisco, CA 94124
800-548-3932
www.abbaka.com

Range hoods in a variety of styles and materials.

American Standard
One Centennial Avenue
Piscataway, NJ 08855-6820
800-223-0068
www.americanstandard-us.com

Offers a full line of kitchen sinks, countertops, and faucets as well as bathroom sinks and fixtures.

Amerock Corp.
4000 Auburn Street
Rockford, IL 61125
815-969-6308
www.amerock.com

Maker of decorative and functional hardware—knobs, pulls, hinges, drawer slides, and more—in a wide range of styles and materials.

Artistic Tile
79 Fifth Avenue
New York, NY 10003
212-727-9331
www.artistictile.com

With several showroom locations, this company features a vast array of tile in ceramic, porcelain, stone, glass, and other materials, as well as a sampling of complementary bath fixtures and accessories.

Asko Inc.
1161 Executive Drive West
Richardson, TX 75081
972-644-8595
www.askousa.com

Best known for European made dishwashers and clothes washers and dryers.

Bates & Bates
3699 Industry Avenue
Lakewood, CA 90721
800-726-7680
www.Batesinks.com

Decorative and specialty plumbing fixtures, including island and bar sinks.

Buddy Rhodes Studio
2130 Oakdale Avenue
San Francisco, CA 94124
877-706-5303
www.buddyrhodes.com

Concrete countertops in varied colors and textures.

C.H. Briggs
P.O. Box 15188
2047 Kutztown Road
Reading, PA 19612
800-355-1000
www.chbriggs.com

A range of decorative hardware—knobs, pulls, and decorative hinges—are offered.

Canac Kitchen & Bath Cabinets
360 John Street
Thornhill, Ontario, Canada L3T 3M9
800-CANAC4U
www.kohlerco.com

The company presents more than 50 door styles and more than 400 styles and finishes in cabinetry.

Canyon Creek Cabinet Co.
16726 Tye Street, SE
Monroe, WA 98272
800-228-1830
www.canyoncreek.com

Semi-custom and custom cabinetry are offered with traditional and European-style construction types available.

Cheng Design/Products
2808 San Pablo Avenue
Berkeley, CA 94702
510-549-2805
www.chengdesign.com

Contemporary style range hoods and modular Geocrete countertops made of concrete available.

Cooper Lighting/Halo
1101 Southerfield Road
Americus, GA 31709
www.cooperlighting.com

The Halo division offers a range of lighting fixtures for the home.

Cosentino USA/Silestone
10707 Corporate Drive, Suite 136
Stafford, TX 77477
281-494-7277
www.cosentinousa.com

Silestone is durable, engineered quartz that comes in a variety of colors and patterns well suited for countertops.

Crossville Porcelain Stone, USA/ Questech Metals
346 Sweeney Drive
Crossville, TN 38555
931-484-2110
www.crossville-ceramics.com

A range of ceramic and porcelain tile for use in the home.

Dacor
950 South Raymond Avenue
Pasadena, CA 91105
800-793-0093
www.dacorappl.com

Residential cooking appliances and ventilation products.

Decora
P.O. Box 420
One Aristokraft Square
Jasper, IN 47547
812-634-2288
www.decoracabinets.com

A range of cabinet styles available through dealers and retailers across the United States.

D.I.G.S.
115 Wooster Street
New York, NY 10012
212-966-7352
www.digs.com

Decorative hardware, bath and home spa products, and home accessory collections.

Dupont Corian
Barley Mill Plaza, Bldg. 12,
Rts. 141 & 48
Wilmington, DE 19805
302-992-2539
www.corian.com

Solid-surfacing material for use in kitchen countertops and backsplashes.

Eliane Ceramic Tiles
2817 Dairy Mick Lane
Dallas, TX 75229
972-481-7854
www.elianeusa.com

A variety of ceramic tile options.

Elkay Manufacturing Co.
2222 Camden Court
Oak Brook, IL 60523
630-574-8484
www.elkay.com

Makers of stainless steel sinks, faucets, waer treatment filters, hot and cold water dispensers, and kitchen accessories.

Franke
3050 Campus Drive, Suite 500
Hatfield, PA 19440
800-626-5873
www.franke.com/ksd

Fine quality sinks, faucets, and kitchen accessories.

Five-Star Division,
Brown Stove Works, Inc.
P.O. Box 2490
Cleveland, TN 37320
423-476-6544
www.fivestarrange.com

Professional-style cooking equipment for the home including gas and dual-fuel ranges, gas cooktops, range hoods, warming drawers, and accessories.

Florim U.S.A.
300 International Boulevard
Clarksville, TN 37040
877-370-5503

Offers imported ceramic and porcelain Italian tile.

Gaggenau/BSH Home Appliances Corp.
5551 McFadden Avenue
Huntington Beach, CA 92649
800-828-9165
www.gaggenau.com/us

High-end, built-in kitchen appliances.

GE Appliances
Appliance Park
Louisville, KY 40225
502-452-3071
www.geappliances.com

A full range of appliances from cooking through refrigeration options.

Grass America
1202 Highway 66 South
Kernersville, NC 27284
800-334-3512
www.grassusa.com

Cabinet hardware for functional use.

Grohe
241 Covington Drive
Bloomingdale, IL 60108
630-583-7711
www.groheamerica.com

A complete line of kitchen and lavatory faucets, including solid stainless steel kitchen pull-outs.

Hafele America Co.
3901 Cheyenne Drive
Archdale, NC 27263-3157
800-423-3531
www.hafeleamericas.com

Decorative hardware, moldings, cabinet accessories, kitchen lighting, slides, hinges, door frames, and other types of storage systems. Hafele is also the U.S. distributor of Ninka organizing systems.

Hettich America
6225 Shiloh Road
Alpharetta, GA 30005
800-HETTICH
www.hettichamerica.com

Makers of functional hardware, cabinet interior drawers systems, and other types of storage and organizational systems for cabinetry.

IAMCO for Faber Range Hoods
P.O. Box 435
Wayland, MA 01778
508-358-5353
www.faberonline.com

Varied styles and types of range hoods.

Kindred Industries Ltd.
1000 Kindred Road
Midland, Ontario, Canada L4R 4K9
705-526-5427
www.kindred-sinkware.com

Stainless steel and color sinks for kitchen, bar, and laundry areas.

KitchenAid
750 Monte Road
Benton Harbor, MI 49022
616-923-5000
www.KitchenAid.com

Full range of large and small kitchen appliances.

Kohler Co.
444 Highland Drive
Kohler, WI 53044
800-4KOHLER
www.kohlerco.com

Kitchen and bath sinks, faucets, fittings, fixtures, and accessories in a wide range of colors, materials, and styles.

KraftMaid Cabinetry
15535 South State Avenue
Middlefield, OH 44062
www.kraftmaid.com

A full range of cabinetry styles and wood species options for kitchen and bath.

LaCornue/Purcell Muray Co.
113 Park Lane
Brisbane, CA 94005
800-892-4040
www.purcellmurray.com

Makers of high-quality kitchen appliances in distinctive styling.

Luceplan USA
315 Hudson Street
New York, NY 10013
212-989-6265
www.luceplan.com

Italian-made lighting fixtures suitable for kitchens and other rooms of the home.

Marvel Industries
P.O. Box 997
Richmond, IN 47375
800-428-6644
www.marvelindustries.com

Premium under-counter built-in refrigeration products, including mini-refrigerators, icemakers, wine and beverage storage, and beer dispensers.

Miele, Inc.
9 Independence Way
Princeton, NJ 08540
800-843-7231
www.miele.com

Makers of cooking and other household appliances, including ovens, dishwashers, and vacuum cleaners.

Nevamar, International Paper
8339 Telegraph Road
Odenton, MD 21113-1397
800-638-4380
www.nevamar.com

High-pressure laminate is offered and available through a network of dealers and distributors.

North River Mint
1520 York Avenue
New York, NY 10028
800-914-9087

Artist-sculpted decorative hardware including knobs and drawer pulls.

Plain & Fancy Custom Cabinetry
Rt. 501 & Oak Street
Schaefferstown, PA 17088
717-949-6571
www.plainfancycabinetry.com

Fine quality cabinetry for kitchens, baths, and home office areas.

St. Charles Cabinetry
215 Diller Avenue
New Holland, PA
717-354-3775
www.stck.com

Cabinetry in contemporary styling for kitchens, baths, and other areas of the home. Part of Heritage Custom Kitchens, makers also of traditional-styled cabinetry.

Snaidero USA
201 W. 132 Street
Los Angeles, CA 90061
877-SNAIDERO
www.snaidero-usa.com

Contemporary designer cabinetry from Italy.

StarMark Inc., A MASCO Company
600 East 48 Street North
Sioux Falls, SD 57104
800-755-7789
www.starmarkcabinetry.com

Makers of custom and semi-custom cabinet lines.

Sub-Zero Freezer Co.
4717 Hammersley Road
Madison, WI 53711
800-444-7820
www.subzero.com

Maker of commercial-style refrigerators and patented refrigerated drawers.

Tile of Spain
2655 Le Jeune Road
Coral Gables, FL 33134
305-446-4387
www.tilespain.com

Fine tile imported from Spain.

Val Cucine NY
152 Wooster Street
New York, NY 10012
212-253-5969
www.valcucineny.com

Makers of fine European-style cabinetry.

Viking Range Corporation
111 Front Street
Greenwood, MS 38930
601-455-1200
www.vikingrange.com

Commercial-style cooking equipment for the home including cooking, refrigeration, and ventilation for indoor and outdoor use.

Vent-A-Hood Ltd.
1000 N. Greenville
Richardson, TX
972-235-5201
www.ventahood.com

Ventilation hoods.

Wilsonart International
2400 Wilson Place
P.O. Box 6110
Temple, TX 76503-6110
800-433-3222
www.wilsonart.com

Surfacing materials, from laminate to solid surfacing in many patterns and colors.

Yorktowne, Inc.
100 Redco Avenue
Red Lion, PA 17356
717-244-4011
www.yorktwn.com

Semi-custom and stock cabinets in a range of wood species, styles, and finishes.

SECTION II DESIGN CREDITS

Warren Ashworth
Bogdanow Partners Architects
75 Spring Street
New York, NY 10012
212-966-0313

("Lofty Ambitions," pages 98-101)

Bruce Bierman
Bruce Bierman Design, Inc.
29 West 15th Street
New York, NY 10011
212-243-1935

("Behind Closed Doors," pages 102-103)

Fu-Tung Cheng
Cheng Design
2808 San Pablo Avenue
Berkeley, CA 94702
510-849-3272

("Penthouse Phenomenon," pages 120-121)

Carol DiCicco Vinci
DiCicco Vinci Architects
135 Fifth Avenue
New York, NY 10010
212-673-5495

("Want to Go Retro?," pages 116-117)

Johnny Grey
Grey & Co. USA
P.O. Box 681
Far Hills, NJ 07931
908-781-1554

("Whimsy in the Kitchen," pages 104-107)

D. Ralph Katz
Timberline Designs
Applegate Farm Complex
Cranbury Station Road
Cranbury, NJ 08512
609-655-9099

("Mixing Woods & Metal," pages 108-109)

Robert Lidsky
The Hammer & Nail
232 Madison Avenue
Wyckoff, NY 07481
201-891-5252

("Repeating Color & Pattern," pages 110-111)

Steven J. Livingston
Studio Snaidero San Francisco
101 Henry Adams St., #400
San Francisco, CA 94103
415-351-1100

("Bungalow Beauty," pages 112-115)

Gary White
Kitchen & Bath Design
1000 Bristrol Street North
Newport Beach, CA 92660
949-955-1232

("The Fire in Metal," pages 118-119)

PHOTO CREDITS

ABAKO: 47, top right

ABBAKA: 28, top left

Abode: 69, right

ALNOPLAN: 43, bottom

American Standard: 60, right

Amerock Corp.: 11, second from right; 51, left

Andrew Bordwin/Bruce Bierman Design: 102-103

Andrew Wood/Interior Archive: 85, bottom left

Artistic Tile: 71, second from bottom and left

Artville Stock: 24, top left and bottom; 25, bottom left

Architer und Wohen, Heiner Orth, Jahreszeiten Verlag: 25, bottom right

Asko: 40

Brady Architectural Photography/NKBA: 52, second from right

Buddy Rhodes Studio: 81

bulthaup GmbH & Cfo.: 90, top and bottom

C.H. Briggs Hardware Co., Inc.: 50, left

Calmenson Comm.: 41, top right

Canyon Creek Cabinet Company: 18; 47

Cheng Products: 30, top; 32, all

Cosentino USA: 54

Cotule: 55, middle

Crate and Barrel: 9, top left; 11, right; 19 right; 23; 64; 66; 68, left and right; 83, bottom right

Crossville Porcelain Stone/USA: 71, top left and right

D.I.G.S.: 51, right

Decora: 73, right

DuPont Corian: 85, top

Ed Reeve/Metro: 19, left; 35; 44, top; 52, second from left; 65, left; 83, bottom left

Eliane Cermaic Tiles: 71, second from top and left

Elizabeth Whiting & Assoc.: 93, third from left, second from right; 122; 125, third from left, second from right.

Ellen Cheever & Associates/Cabinets by St. Charles: 29, 44, bottom right; 49; 62; 71, top; 73, bottom; 75, 85, bottom right

Eric Roth: 27; 53, bottom left; 65, right; 78; 79; 80, left, 83, top right

Florim USA: 71, bottom

Forgings: 51, left

Franke: 56

Frederick Charles/Warren Ashworth, Bogdanow Partners Architects, PC: 98-101

Fritz von der Schulenberg/Interior Archive: 77, bottom; 93, right; 96, bottom right; 123, top; 125, right

Gaggenau: 33, top; 38; 41, left

GE Appliances: 30, middle; 33, bottom; 37; 41, top left and bottom

Grass America: 66, bottom left

Grey Crawford/Beateworks: 9, bottom; 83, top left; 90, middle right; 93, left, second from left; 94-95; 96, top and left (Courtesy of Taunton Press); 123, bottom; 125, left, second from left

Grohe: 60, left; 63

Häfele America Co.: 50, right; 67, second from bottom

Heritage/St. Charles Cabinetry: 20;

Hettich America: 67, top and second from top

Iamco/Faber: 30, bottom

Ikea: 12; 13; 17, top; 66, bottom right

James Bingnear, Stuart Kitchens/Heritage Custom Kitchens: 20, right

Jay Graham/Stephen Livingston, Snaidero Kitchens ı Design: 112 115

Jeff Frey & Associates/NKBA: 36, top; 39, left

John Martinelli/D. Ralph Katz, Timberline Design: 108-109

Johnny Grey Company: 104-107

Kevin Thomas: 24, top right and bottom right; 25, top left and right

Kindred Industries: 59

Kitchen Smith, Inc. Design/Heritage Custom Kitchens: 86

KitchenAid: 36, bottom right

Kitchens by Deane/Heritage Custom Kitchens: 80, right

Klaff's Inc.: 69

Kohler Co.: 58; 62, bottom

La Cornue/Parcell Murray Co.: 31, left

Larry A. Falke/Gary White, Kitchen & Bath Design 118-119

Leucos: 88, left

Luceplan USA Inc.: 87

© Marvel Industries: 68, middle

Matthew Millman: 31, right; 61, top; 120-121, Cheng Design

Miele, Inc.: 33, bottom; 38

Nadia MacKenzie/Interior Archive: 23

Neil Kelly Cabinets: 73, left

Nevamar International Paper: 53, top

Ninka: 67, bottom

North River Mint: 51, middle

Northlight Photography Inc./NKBA: 42

Peter Cameron Design/Cabinets by St. Charles: 16, bottom; 17, bottom, 52, left and right

Peter Raymond/Robert Lidsky, The Hammer & Nail, Inc.: 110

Plain & Fancy Cabinetry: 21; 44, bottom right; 66, top right;

Raymond Kranz, Design Studio West/Heritage Custom Kitchens: 14; 43, top

Robert Blosser/DiCicco Vinci Architects 116-117

Sam Kulla, Kulla Kitchens/Heritage Custom Kitchens: 28, bottom left and right

Sarah Reep, StarMark/Cabinets by St. Charles: 15; 16, top

Snaidero: 47, top left

Sub-Zero Freezer Co.: 47, bottom right; 66, top left

Tile of Spain: 71, second from top and right

Tim Street-Porter/Beateworks: 76; 77, top; 90, left

Transolid: 57

Viking Culinary Arts Center/Ellen Cheever & Associates Design/Photo Courtesy of St. Charles: 9, top right; 84

Viking Range Corp: 36, bottom left

Yorktowne, Inc.: 46

INDEX

ACKNOWLEDGMENTS

Though the author's name goes on the cover, there are many professionals behind the scenes who make a book possible. Topping the list for me is Francine Hornberger, Hornberger Publishing Services, who is the best guide and coach an author can have. Kudos as well to the outstanding editorial and production team at Rockport Publishers: Shawna Mullen, Martha Wetherill, Jay Donahue, Kristy Mulkern, Cora Hawks, Betsy Gammons, and Susan Raymond. Like gem cutters taking raw materials from the earth and transforming them into quality jewels, full of light and color, this team has done so for *The Modern Kitchen Workbook*.

Chen Design Associates are the graphic artists—wizards really—who blended beautifully the science of information and detail with the artistry of attractive presentation. Now, onto some of the people who made the ideas and photos happen. Fu-Tung Cheng is a designer, builder, artist, and visionary. In addition to his design firm, Cheng Design in Berkeley, California, he is filling a niche in the industry with his product division, Cheng Products, which debuted by offering contemporary range hoods and has expanded to include modular concrete countertops. Thank you, Fu-Tung, for contributing your wisdom in the Foreword and design vision in the Ideabook section.

Heartfelt thanks to these fine designers who allowed me to share their work in the case studies presented: Johnny Grey, Johnny Grey & Co.; Robert Lidsky, The Hammer & Nail; Steven Livingston, Studio Snaidero San Francisco; D. Ralph Katz, Timberline Designs; Carol DiCicco Vinci, DiCicco Vinci Architects; Gary White, CKD, CBD, CID, Kitchen & Bath Design; Bruce Bierman, Bruce Bierman Design Inc.; Warren Ashworth, Bogdanow Partners Architects PC; and The National Kitchen & Bath Association (NKBA) each year holds an annual competition that honors the outstanding work of its kitchen and bath dealer/designer members. Thanks to the NKBA for allowing publication of winning projects by these designers: Rebecca Lindquist, CKD, CBD, and Tina Marie Sell, Lindquist & Co. (photo on p. 36, top); Diana Valentine, CKD, Distinctive Kitchens & Baths (photo on p. 44, right); and Leslie Cohen, CKD, Leslie Cohen Design (p. 52, third photo from left). Thanks to Ellen Cheever, Ellen Cheever & Associates, who shared the treasure trove of projects using St. Charles and Heritage Custom Kitchens cabinetry designed by these professionals as well as herself: Reymond Kranz, Design Studio West; Sarah Reep, StarMark; Peter Cameron Design; James Bingnear, Stuart Kitchens; Sam Kulla, Kulla Kitchens; Kitchens By Deane; and Kitchen Smith Inc. Design.

Working at *Kitchen & Bath Business* magazine has allowed me to gather information from its archives, and draw inspiration from professionals in the field with rare and relative ease. I am grateful for the opportunity to have been a part of that fine publication.

Your kitchen would be just another empty space without the fine products created by manufacturers today to fill it. Companies who contributed product photography to this book are listed in the Resources Directory. Here, I extend my gratitude to them for their cooperation and for their dedication to making our homes comfortable, functional, and pretty places to live.

Thanks goes to you, dear reader, for spending time with all of us who fashioned this book. We hope that armed with the knowledge contained here, you will create a kitchen to be the place you want it to be!

ABOUT THE AUTHOR

Wanda Jankowski is publisher and editor-in-chief of *Kitchen & Bath Business*, the leading trade magazine of the kitchen and bath industry, and its sister publication, *Luxury Kitchens & Baths*. Her career as a journalist in the design and building fields includes having served also as editor-in-chief of *Architectural Lighting*, *Designers' Kitchens & Baths*, *Build It! Home Plans*, *Build It! Ultra*, and *Lighting Design & Application*.

This is Ms. Jankowski's seventh book. Other titles include: *Bathrooms: Designs for Living*, *Creative Lighting: Custom and Decorative Luminaires*, *Kitchens & Baths: Designs for Living*, *Designing with Light: Residential Interiors*, *Lighting: Exteriors & Landscapes*, and *The Best of Lighting Design*. Originally from Brooklyn, New York, Ms. Jankowski currently resides in Manhattan.